T0356295

THE CHARISMATIC LEADER

THE CHARISMATIC LEADER

21 Skills to Connect with People

JOHN C. MAXWELL

HARPERCOLLINS
LEADERSHIP

AN IMPRINT OF HARPERCOLLINS

PUBLISHING

Published by HarperCollins Leadership, an imprint of HarperCollins Focus LLC.

Published in association with Yates & Yates, www.yates2.com.

Any internet addresses, phone numbers, or company or product information printed in this book are offered as a resource and are not intended in any way to be or to imply an endorsement by HarperCollins, nor does HarperCollins vouch for the existence, content, or services of these sites, phone numbers, companies, or products beyond the life of this book.

ISBN 978-1-4003-4692-9 (HC)
ISBN 978-1-4003-4697-4 (eBook)
ISBN 978-1-4003-4698-1 (digital audio)

Printed in the United States of America

24 25 26 27 28 LBC 5 4 3 2 1

CONTENTS

PART 2: BECOME INVESTED IN PEOPLE

PART 3: BECOME INTERESTING TO PEOPLE

ACKNOWLEDGMENT

Thank you to Charlie Wetzel for his help in preparing this book.

INTRODUCTION:
WHAT IS CHARISMA?

What is charisma? And does every leader need it?

Let's start with the second question first. Leadership is influence—nothing more, nothing less. What's the significance of that truth? It means that leading *always* involves working with people. And it's a fact that everyone is more willing to *go* along with people they *get* along with. So if you want to lead people well, using influence instead of resorting to pressure or coercion, you must become a likeable person and make yourself approachable and attractive to others. Having charisma makes people *want* to spend time with you, work with you, and accomplish worthwhile objectives together with you.

Are some people born with natural charisma, who have an innate ability to attract others? The answer is yes—there's no denying it. The people at Gallop who developed StrengthFinder call it WOO: the ability to win over others. If you possess that ability, that's great. But if you don't, here's good news. Charisma is like leadership. It can be learned and developed. No matter how much or how little leadership talent you naturally possess, you can develop it and become a better leader. Likewise, no matter how much or how little natural charisma you possess, you can learn to be more charismatic and develop the ability to become more likeable.

What's the secret to charisma? It's actually very simple: focusing on others. To be charismatic, you don't need to be physically attractive, tall, athletic, talented, or rich. You just need to care about people and make them feel important. Anyone who does that can connect with people and become a shining light in a dreary world.

Frederick L. Collins said, "Always remember there are two types of people in the world: those who come into a room and say, 'Here I am!' and those that come in and say, 'Ah, there you are!'"[1] The essence of charisma is the ability to think *There you are!* with everyone you meet and to take actions that let them know they're important. If you do that, you will be able to connect with them.

> "There are two types of people in the world: those who come into a room and say, 'Here I am!' and those that come in and say, 'Ah, there you are!'"
>
> —FREDERICK L. COLLINS

In this book, I will walk you through twenty-one simple ways to develop charisma by interacting positively with people. You'll learn skills in three phases:

1. Becoming Interested in Others
2. Becoming Invested in Others
3. Becoming Interesting to Others

Charisma starts with becoming interested in others. When you care about people and learn about them, they will find *you* interesting. From there, you will learn simple ways to invest in others to add value to them. Finally, you will learn four ways to make yourself more interesting. This is where most people mistakenly try to begin developing charisma, but it is, in fact, the least important of the three. To become charismatic, make yourself about others.

If you will take the time to practice these simple skills with others every day, people will seek you out and want to engage with you. You will connect with them. And you will receive greater opportunities to add value to them, lead them, and create success for everyone.

PART 1

BECOME INTERESTED IN PEOPLE

PUT YOUR FOCUS ON OTHERS

I don't know what your destiny will be, but one thing I
know: the only ones among you who will be really happy
are those who have sought and found how to serve.

—ALBERT SCHWEITZER

Truly charismatic people care about others and focus their attention on them, not on themselves. In my book *Winning with People*, I discuss the Big Picture Principle, which states: "The entire population of the world—with one minor exception—is composed of other people."[1] We must get outside of ourselves, see the bigger picture, and start putting other people first if we want to live our best life and become better leaders. Everyone else in the world matters, not just us.

If you've never thought of life in those terms, then it's time to give it a try. When individuals think of themselves as the center of the universe, not only are they in for a big disappointment when they discover it's not true, but they'll also alienate themselves from everyone around them. That makes it difficult to lead people. I've never met a person who works well with people who has not mastered the ability to keep their eyes off the mirror and serve others with dignity.

> "The entire population of the world—with one minor exception—is composed of other people."
>
> —THE BIG PICTURE PRINCIPLE

HOW FOCUSING ON OTHERS HELPS *YOU*

Most people would readily admit that unselfishness is a positive quality, and even the most egocentric individual possesses the desire, deep down, to help others. The problem, sometimes, is changing our behavior so that we get in the habit of focusing on others instead of on ourselves. Here are three thoughts to help you remember to keep your focus on other people where it really belongs:

1. FOCUSING ON OTHERS WILL GIVE YOU A SENSE OF PURPOSE

If you like to stream old black-and-white TV shows, you may have come across Danny Thomas, the entertainer who starred in *Make Room for Daddy*. Thomas observed, "All of us are born for a reason, but all of us don't discover why. Success in life has nothing to do with what you gain in life or accomplish for yourself. It's what you do for others."[2]

Not only did Thomas believe that, but he also lived it. As a successful entertainer and television star, he could have done nothing but enjoy the benefits of his achievement. But he desired something more. He founded St. Jude's Hospital, a research facility that focuses on treating children who suffer from catastrophic diseases. And Thomas dedicated much of his life to supporting it. It helped him enjoy a greater purpose.

Put your focus on others, and a greater purpose for your life and leadership may reveal itself.

2. FOCUSING ON OTHERS CAN GIVE YOU ENERGY

Continual focus on yourself will drain you of energy. In contrast, focusing on others usually has the opposite effect. My friend Bill McCartney knew this back when he was head football coach for the University of Colorado Buffaloes in the 1980s and early 1990s. Coach Mac had heard that most people spend 86 percent of their time thinking about themselves, but only 14 percent of their time thinking about others. Yet he knew instinctively that if his players focused their attention on people they cared about instead of just on themselves, a whole new source of energy would be available to them.

In 1991 Coach Mac decided to use this information when he was facing a great challenge. Colorado was scheduled to play its archrival, the Nebraska Cornhuskers, on Nebraska's home turf. The problem was that Colorado had not won a game there in twenty-three years. But Coach McCartney believed in his team and looked for a way to inspire them to achieve. In the end, he decided to appeal to their love of others. He did it by challenging each player to call an individual he loved and tell that person he was dedicating the game to him or her. Coach Mac also encouraged the players to ask that person to watch every play, knowing that every hit, every tackle, every block, and every score was being dedicated to him or her.

Coach Mac took one more step. He arranged to distribute sixty footballs with the game's final score written on them, so that each player could send a ball to the individual he had chosen. The result? The Colorado Buffaloes won the game. The final score written on the footballs was "27 to 12."

3. FOCUSING ON OTHERS CAN GIVE YOU A SENSE OF CONTENTMENT

I'm told that psychological research shows that people are better adjusted and more likely to feel content if they serve others. Serving others cultivates health and brings about happiness. People have instinctively known that for centuries—even before the science of psychology was formally developed. For example, look at the wisdom (and humor) found in this time-honored proverb:

If you want happiness for an hour—take a nap.
If you want happiness for a day—go fishing.
If you want happiness for a month—get married.
If you want happiness for a year—inherit a fortune.
If you want happiness for a lifetime—help others.

It may seem counterintuitive, but by focusing on others, you not only help them, but you also *help yourself.* You feel better about who you are and what you do. You help the people you focus on to feel better about themselves and perform better. You increase your influence with them. And you make the world a better place. Who doesn't want all that?

If you want happiness for a lifetime— help others.

BELIEVE THE BEST OF OTHERS

To err is human; to forgive is not company policy.

—UNKNOWN

Anybody can see weaknesses, mistakes, and shortcomings in other people. That takes no unique skill. Seeing only the good things in them is much harder, but it has so many positive benefits. Hall of Fame baseball player Reggie Jackson pointed out the power that ability has in developing and leading others. He observed, "A great manager has a knack for making ballplayers think they are better than they think they are. He forces you to have a good opinion of yourself. He lets you know he believes in you. He makes you get more out of yourself. And once you learn how good you really are, you never settle for playing anything less than your very best."[1]

What Jackson described can be applied to any area of life, not just baseball. It works in business, parenting, marriage, and volunteer work. If you want people to be drawn to you, don't look for the flaws, warts, and blemishes in others. Look for their best.

I've found that when I am suspicious of others, it causes me to display wrong behavior toward them. And it makes any interaction with them worse. In general, you get what you expect from others. I have chosen to take the high road, expect the best, and be blessed most of the time.

I had this practice modeled to me by my mother when I was growing up. Mom knew my heart and she always evaluated my behavior in light of it. Like every other kid, I got my fair share of reprimands. And I deserved them. But Mom never seemed to jump to conclusions with me. She never assumed the worst. Instead, she always assumed the best. And that's key to cultivating this quality.

HOW TO EXPECT THE BEST

Believing the best about others and extending them grace and forgiveness is a very winning quality that will make you attractive to other people. To cultivate it, do the following:

LOOK FOR THE BEST ABOUT PEOPLE

If you want to believe the best in others, then the first thing you need to do is check your attitude. How do you see people? Do you believe that, deep down, people desire to be good, to do their best? That matters, because if you don't believe the best in others, you will never believe that their intentions are good. And if you don't believe in their intentions, you will start making negative assumptions about them and treat them poorly.

Instead, actively *look* for the best in them. Search for their best traits. Catch them doing what's right and compliment them for it. When you assume the best and look for it, it becomes much easier to maintain a positive attitude toward people.

SEE THINGS FROM OTHERS' PERSPECTIVE

Seeing things from the perspective of others takes maturity. The less mature one is, the more difficult it is to see things from another's point of view. Think about the biblical story of the woman caught in adultery where Jesus challenged the people without sin to cast the first stone. The *oldest* people in the crowd were the first to drop their stones and walk away.[2] Why? Their maturity gave them better perspective.

"Since we tend to see ourselves primarily in light of our *intentions*, which are invisible to others," said philosopher J. G. Bennett, "while we see others mainly in the light of their *actions*, which are all that's visible to us, we have a situation in which misunderstanding and injustice are the order of the day."[3] When you assume people's intentions are good, you extend grace to them, and that makes you much more approachable and attractive as a person.

GIVE PEOPLE THE BENEFIT OF THE DOUBT

When you were a child, perhaps you were taught the Golden Rule: "Do unto others as you would have them do unto you." I've often found that when my intentions were right but my actions turned out wrong, I wanted others to see me in light of the Golden Rule. In other words, I wanted others to give me the benefit of the doubt. Why shouldn't I try to extend the same courtesy to others?

Frank Clark commented, "What great accomplishments we would have in the world if everybody had done what they intended to do." While I'd agree that's true, I'd also add, "What great relationships we would have if everybody was appreciated for what they intended to do—in spite of how things turned out." When you give someone the benefit of the doubt, you are following the most effective interpersonal rule that has ever been written.

FOCUS ON PEOPLE'S GOOD DAYS, NOT THEIR BAD ONES

We all have good days and bad days. I don't know about you, but I'd like to be remembered for my good ones. And I can only ask to be forgiven for my bad ones. Fuller Theological Seminary professor David Augsburger observed, "Since nothing we intend is ever faultless . . . and nothing we achieve without some measure of finitude and fallibility we call humanness, we are saved by forgiveness."[4] If you desire to believe the best of others, then forgiveness is essential. And it's rarely a one-time thing. Civil rights leader Martin Luther King Jr. was right when he said, "Forgiveness is not an occasional act; it is a permanent attitude."[5]

If you didn't grow up in a loving supportive home like I did, you may find it challenging to believe the best in others because maybe no one believed the best of you. But when it comes right down to it, giving others the benefit of the doubt and believing the best of them is a choice. And I've seen a lot of people who grew up with few advantages rise above their situation and become winners in every sense of the word. That gives everyone hope. And remember, the way you judge others will be the one used to judge you. If you believe the best of others in every one of your relationships, then people will more likely do the same for you.

> "Since nothing we intend is ever faultless, and nothing we achieve without some measure of finitude and fallibility we call humanness, we are saved by forgiveness."
>
> —DAVID AUGSBURGER

ADD VALUE TO PEOPLE

Try not to become a man of success, but
rather try to become a man of value.

—ALBERT EINSTEIN

The day I graduated from college and was only weeks away from going to my first leadership position, I talked to my father and asked him to give me the best advice he could for my career.

"Son," Dad replied, "value people, believe in them, and love them unconditionally. Do those things every day, and you will be successful." I didn't think of it this way at the time, but what he was really doing was explaining how I could develop charisma with people.

> "Value people, believe in them, and love them unconditionally. Do those things every day, and you will be successful."
>
> —MELVIN MAXWELL

That advice set the course for me, not only in my career, but also in my personal life. That was the day that I made adding value to people my goal, and it's something I've striven to do every day for the past fifty-five years.

THREE WAYS TO ADD VALUE

At the core of my being, I believe that nothing in this life is more important than people, and we should do everything in our power to add value to people. If you desire to become a value adder, then take these things to heart:

1. VALUE PEOPLE

Your ability to add value *to* people starts with your attitude *toward* people. Human relations expert Les Giblin remarked, "You can't make the other fellow feel important in your presence if you secretly feel that he is a nobody."[1] Isn't that true? Don't you find it difficult to do something kind for someone when you dislike them?

The way we see people is often the difference between manipulating and motivating them. If we don't want to help people, but we want them to help us, then we get in trouble. We manipulate people when we move them for our *personal* advantage. However, we motivate people when we move them for *mutual* advantage. Adding value to others is often a win-win proposition.

> "You can't make the other fellow feel important in your presence if you secretly feel that he is a nobody."
>
> —LES GIBLIN

How do you see people? Are they potential recipients of value you can give, or do they tend to be nuisances along your desired path to success? Author Sydney J. Harris said, "People want to be appreciated, not impressed. They want to be regarded as human beings, not as sounding boards for other people's egos. They want to be treated as an end in themselves, not as a means towards the gratification of another's vanity."[2] If you want to add value to people, you must value them first.

2. MAKE YOURSELF MORE VALUABLE

Have you ever heard the phrase "You cannot give what you do not have"? There are people who possess good hearts and the desire to give, yet they have very little to offer. Why? Because they have not first added value to themselves. Making yourself more valuable is not an entirely selfish act. When you acquire knowledge, learn a new skill, or gain experience, you not only improve yourself, but you also increase your ability to add value to others.

In 1974 I committed myself to the pursuit of personal growth. I knew that it would help me to be a better leader, so I began to continually read books, listen to tapes, attend conferences, and learn from better leaders. At the time, I had no idea that this commitment would be the most important thing I would ever do to help others. But that has turned out to be the case. As I improve myself, I am better able to help others improve. The more I grow, the more I can help others grow. The same will be true for you. If you want to add value to people, you must make yourself more valuable.

3. KNOW WHAT PEOPLE VALUE

Have you ever been given a gift that didn't suit you or that you could not use? Perhaps the giver was so self-focused that they gave a gift *they* would like. Or maybe the giver didn't know you and missed the mark. If so, while you may have been grateful for the effort they made, the gift didn't really help you.

That's what it can be like for people when you try to add value to them without knowing who they are or what they value. Once we know what people value, with some effort we can add value to them. That's why I pay attention and note what the people in my life value, including family members, friends, colleagues, employees, and leaders who engage me as a speaker. If you do likewise, you'll not only help people more, but you'll also raise your likeability factor.

When you add value to people, you earn the right to do so much more for them. You can lift them up, help them advance, make them a part of something bigger than themselves, and help them to become who they are made to be. And when you're a person's leader, you may be in the best position to help them to do those things.

To become good at adding value to others, you must become highly intentional about it. Why do I say that? Because human beings are naturally selfish. I'm selfish. Being

> **When you add value to people, you earn the right to do so much more for them.**

someone who adds value requires me to get out of my comfort zone every day and think about specific ways to add value to others. But that's what it takes to be a more charismatic leader whom others want to follow.

4

ENCOURAGE OTHERS
EVERY TIME YOU MEET

He who waits to do a great deal of good
at once, will never do anything.

—SAMUEL JOHNSON

As a child and young man, I learned a lot of lessons about likability from watching my father. One of those came from the way he encouraged everyone he met. When he was the president of what is today Ohio Christian University, I would often walk across the campus with him. He continually stopped to talk with students. When I became frustrated and was tempted to complain, I would look at the students' faces and realize Dad was depositing good words inside of them. Within the first thirty seconds of a conversation, he always made it his goal to say something positive and encouraging to them. As I imitated him and learned this skill, I started to think of it as the thirty-second rule.

That kind of treatment of others made my father very charismatic to others. For many years, many of his former students used to travel from all over the United States to visit him in Florida. He was surprised that they would go out of their way to see him, but I wasn't. Dad was an incredible leader. Everyone loved him.

EVERYONE NEEDS ENCOURAGEMENT

Someone once said to me, "Be kind because everyone you meet is fighting a hard battle." I think that's true. People everywhere need a good word or an uplifting compliment to fire their hopes and dreams. It takes very little effort to do, but it really lifts people up. Here's how:

1. ENCOURAGEMENT SHOWS YOU CARE

Every day before I meet with people, I pause to think about something encouraging I can tell them. What I say can be one of many things: I might thank them for something they've done for me or a friend. I might tell others about one of their accomplishments. I might praise them for a personal quality they exhibit. Or I might simply compliment their appearance. The practice isn't complicated, but it does take some time, effort, and discipline. The reward for practicing it is huge because it really makes a positive impact on people. When you're thoughtful enough to plan a kindness, they know you really care about them.

2. ENCOURAGING OTHERS GIVES THEM THE TRIPLE-A TREATMENT

All people feel better and do better when you give them *attention, affirmation,* and *appreciation*. The next time you make contact with people, begin by giving them your undivided attention when you first meet them. Affirm them and show your appreciation for them in some way. Then watch what happens. You will be surprised by how positively they respond. And if you have trouble remembering to keep your focus on them instead of on yourself, then perhaps the words of William King will help you. He quipped, "A gossip is one who talks to you about other people. A bore is one who talks to you about himself. And a brilliant conversationalist is one who talks to you about yourself."

3. ENCOURAGEMENT GIVES OTHERS ENERGY

Psychologist Henry H. Goddard conducted a study on energy levels in children using an instrument he called the "ergograph." His findings are fascinating. He discovered that when tired children were given a word of praise or commendation, the ergograph showed an immediate upward surge of energy in the children. When the children were criticized or discouraged, the ergograph showed that their physical energy took a sudden nosedive.[1]

You may have already discovered

> "A gossip is one who talks to you about other people. A bore is one who talks to you about himself. And a brilliant conversationalist is one who talks to you about yourself."
>
> —WILLIAM KING

this intuitively. When someone praises you, doesn't your energy level go up? And when you are criticized, doesn't that comment drag you down? Words have great power.

What kind of environment do you think you could create if you continually affirmed people when you first came into contact with them? Not only would you encourage them, but you would also become an energy carrier. Whenever you walked into a room, the people would light up when they saw you. You would help to create the kind of environment everyone loves. Just your presence alone would brighten people's day. That's charisma.

4. ENCOURAGEMENT INCREASES OTHERS' MOTIVATION

Vince Lombardi, the famed Green Bay Packers football coach, was a feared disciplinarian. But he was also a great motivator. One day he chewed out a player who had missed several blocking assignments. After practice, Lombardi stormed into the locker room and saw that the player was sitting at his locker, head down, dejected. Lombardi mussed his hair, patted him on the shoulder, and said, "One of these days, you're going to be the best guard in the NFL."[2]

That player was Jerry Kramer, and Kramer says he carried that positive image of himself for the rest of his career. "Lombardi's encouragement had a tremendous impact on my whole life,"[3] Kramer said. He went on to become a member of the Green Bay Packers Hall of Fame and a member of the NFL's 50th Anniversary All-Time Team.

Everybody needs motivation from time to time, and when they receive it, that encouragement really helps them:

- Motivation helps people who know what they should do . . . to do it!
- Motivation helps people who know what commitment they should make . . . to make it!
- Motivation helps people who know what habit they should break . . . to break it!
- Motivation helps people who know what path they should take . . . to take it!

Motivation makes it possible to accomplish what they want to accomplish.

One of my favorite encouragement quotes can be found in a letter written by founding father Benjamin Franklin to revolutionary naval commander John Paul Jones. He wrote:

Hereafter, if you should observe an occasion to give your officers and friends a little more praise than is their due, and confess more fault than you can justly be charged with, you will only become the sooner for it a great captain. Criticizing and censuring almost everyone you have to do with, will diminish friends, encrease enemies, and thereby hurt your affairs.[4]

In other words, treating others negatively *lowers* your level of charisma and diminishes your leadership while encouraging others *raises* it. So, if you want to improve your relationships with others and create a positive atmosphere for yourself and your team, encourage others every time you meet.

5

REMEMBER PEOPLE'S NAMES

Remember that a person's name is to that person the
sweetest and most important sound in any language.

—DALE CARNEGIE

In 1937 the granddaddy of all people-skills books was published. It was an overnight hit, eventually selling more than thirty million copies.[1] That book was *How to Win Friends and Influence People,* by Dale Carnegie. What made it so valuable was Carnegie's understanding of human nature. The book is a course in charisma.

When I was a kid, my father paid me to read books instead of giving me an allowance, and this was one of the books he paid me to read. It made quite an impression on me. I loved Carnegie's simple words of wisdom. Something that I learned from Carnegie was this: remember and use a person's name. He wrote,

> We should be aware of the *magic* contained in a name and realize that this single item is wholly owned by the person with whom we are dealing . . . and nobody else. The name sets the individual apart; it makes him or her unique among all others. The information we are imparting or the request we are making

takes on a special importance when we approach the situation with the name of the individual. From the waiter to the executive, the name will work magic as we deal with others."[2]

From the time I first read those words when I was in junior high school, I made it a point to learn and remember people's names.

A PERSONAL TOUCH IS NEEDED NOW MORE THAN EVER

What was true in 1937 is even more applicable in our fast-paced world. People are more isolated and unseen today than ever before. Others identify them by an account number or a username, and as a result they feel unacknowledged and unappreciated. Remembering a person's name and calling them by it tells them you care about them as an individual.

Too many leaders fail to treat people like individuals. Instead, they approach their team as if it were a single nameless entity, or worse, they see only the function of the team, and treat the group not like individual people, but as they would a machine or a tool for their own purpose and advancement. Learning someone's name, remembering it, and using it—especially in a large organization—demonstrates that you value people and care enough about them to make the effort to get to know them.

If you want to improve your relationships with people and increase your likeability, remember people's names. Here are a few tips to help you:

MAKE THE DECISION TO VALUE AND LEARN NAMES

People value their names and always have. Playwright William Shakespeare wrote,

> Good name in man and woman, dear my lord,
> Is the immediate jewel of their souls:
> Who steals my purse steals trash; 'tis something,
>   nothing;
> 'Twas mine, 'tis his, and has been slave to
>   thousands.
> But he that filches from me my good name
> Robs me of that which not enriches him
> And makes me poor indeed.[3]

Think about how you value your own name. How do you feel when someone calls you by the wrong name? How about when you kindly correct the person and spend time with them, and they still get your name wrong? In contrast, how about when people haven't seen you for a long time, and they still remember your name? Doesn't it make you feel good? (And doesn't it also impress you?) When people care enough to know your name, they make you feel valued.

> "Good name in man and woman . . . is the immediate jewel of their souls."
>
> —WILLIAM SHAKESPEARE

Most people don't naturally remember everyone's names. It takes intentionality. Decide to make the effort.

USE THE "SAVE" METHOD TO REMEMBER NAMES

My friend Jerry Lucas, an Ohio State basketball legend and NBA Hall of Famer, was known as "Dr. Memory." He spent the years following his hugely successful run in the NBA helping schoolchildren and adults improve their memories through a variety of innovative techniques. One of the things he taught is called the SAVE Method. Here's how it works:

S—Say the name three times in conversation.

A—Ask a question about the name (for example, how it is spelled) or about the person.

V—Visualize the person's prominent physical or personality feature.

E—End the conversation with the name.[4]

I've used similar techniques to remember names and they really work. Years ago, Jerry demonstrated his ability to remember names using this technique on the old *Tonight Show* hosted by Johnny Carson. Before the show, Jerry met every guest who would be in the audience that night and memorized every name of every person. During the show, he was able to recall every name. Try the SAVE method and see if it works for you.

WHEN YOU CAN'T EASILY REMEMBER A NAME . . .

Almost everyone has trouble recalling names on some occasions. When this happens, try to recall the situation in which you met the person or last saw them. If you can't recall even that, then ask, "How long has it been?" Perhaps that will jog your memory.

If you're meeting people along with a friend or colleague, sometimes you can help each other out. Introduce the person whose name you do remember to the person whose name you don't, and perhaps the other individual will volunteer his name. Or you can agree with your friend ahead of time to come to each other's aid. My wife and I do this. When we make introductions, Margaret knows that if I don't introduce someone by name, I'm not sure I remember it correctly. And she will quickly introduce herself and get the other person's name in return.

When all else fails, just say, "I'm so sorry; I remember you, but I'm afraid your name has slipped my mind." Then after the individual reminds you, use the SAVE method so that you are less likely to forget it again in the future.

GIVE YOURSELF GRACE IF YOU FORGET

If you work at it, you *will* become better at remembering people's names, but don't be too hard on yourself when you blow it. That's what I did recently when meeting a couple whose last name was Lake. One of the things I do when learning a name is to link the name to a mental image. When I was introduced to the Lakes, I immediately placed a mental image of a lake on their heads and thought of Hargus Lake where I grew up. A few days later when I saw them again, I mistakenly asked, "How are you doing tonight, Mr. and Mrs. Hargus?" Sometimes even our best practices fail us!

If you make the effort to remember names and are successful even only part of the time, the people's whose names you remember will appreciate you, and even the ones whose names you can't recall will sense that you care about them and desire to know them better. Your attitude will shine through, and you will be more attractive to others.

6

LEARN WHAT MATTERS
TO PEOPLE

Coaches who can outline plays on a blackboard are
a dime a dozen. The ones who succeed are those
who get inside their players and motivate them.

—VINCE LOMBARDI

In the 1980s, I had the privilege, along with about thirty other leaders, to spend two days with the father of modern management, Peter Drucker. One of the things he said was, "Leading people is like conducting an orchestra. There are many different players and instruments that the conductor must know thoroughly." Drucker challenged us to *really* know the key players on our team. I really took that to heart and became highly intentional about learning who people were and what really mattered to them.

WHAT'S IMPORTANT TO YOU IS IMPORTANT TO ME

When you take the time to learn what is important to others and you make that important to you, it communicates how much you care and desire to develop a good relationship with others. And it makes you appreciate them more and accept them more readily for who they are. As I've made the effort to get to know people better over the last forty years, here are a few things I've learned along the way:

ACCEPT THE FACT THAT PEOPLE ARE DIFFERENT

I've written in previous books about how, when I was young, I used to believe that everyone ought to be like me to be more successful. I've matured quite a bit since then. Florence Littauer's book *Personality Plus* was eye-opening to me and helped me a lot.[1] I experienced more growth as I traveled and met many kinds of people. I now recognize the major gaps in my skills and abilities. I appreciate people with different talents and temperaments. I understand that people have very different life experiences from mine, and many people haven't had the benefits I have. All that makes me much more open-minded and appreciative of differences.

As you set out to learn what's important to others, I want to caution you not to judge them. Instead, value them, accept them unconditionally, and appreciate their differences. Everyone is important and has value. And what they care about matters.

ASK QUESTIONS TO LEARN ABOUT PEOPLE

It may seem fundamental, but asking a good question is essential to discovering what makes people tick and what matters to them most. Through the years, I have developed a list of questions that have helped me in this endeavor time and time again. You may want to use them too:

- **"What do you dream about?"** You can learn about people's minds by looking at what they have already achieved, but to understand their hearts, look at what they dream of becoming.

- **"What do you cry about?"** When you understand people's pain, you can't help but understand their hearts.

- **"What do you sing about?"** What brings people joy is often a source of their strength.

- **"What are your values?"** When people give you access to their values, know that you have entered the most sacred chambers of their hearts.

- **"What are your strengths?"** Whatever people perceive as their strengths makes their hearts proud.

- **"What is your temperament?"** Learn that, and you often discover the way to their hearts.

Obviously, you don't want your questions to feel like an interview, and you don't need to find out all the answers in one sitting. The process can be natural while being intentional. Be curious. Ask questions. Listen and learn.

ESTABLISH COMMON GROUND

Our English word *communication* comes from the Latin word *communis*, which means "common." Effective leaders, communicators, and people persons always find something they have in common with the people they are speaking to. This makes them more charismatic. It is on common ground that they connect with others. If you've asked questions and listened, then you will have discovered common ground.

Sometimes in meetings, hidden agendas can make communication ineffective because they make it difficult for people to meet on common ground. When that happens, try suggesting that all parties agree to a simple ground rule. When one person disagrees with another, before he's allowed to make his own point, he has to understand and be able to articulate his opponent's point. You would be amazed at how quickly this practice puts people on common ground.

REALIZE THAT WITH TIME, PEOPLE CHANGE

It is a major leap for some people to tune into others' dreams and desires and to discover what matters most to them. But it's not enough to do that with a person only once and then assume you've "got it" forever. Time changes all things, including the human heart. Think of learning about people as an ongoing dialog that occurs over the lifetime of the relationship.

Fred Bucy, former president of Texas Instruments, observed, "It is much easier to assume that what worked yesterday will work today, and this is simply not true."[2] What's effective in inspiring and motivating people at one point in their careers will not necessarily be effective later. What touches people's hearts at one stage of life often changes as they grow older. Successes and failures, tragedies and triumphs, goals achieved and dreams laid to rest all make an impact on a person's values and desires.

> "It is much easier to assume that what worked yesterday will work today, and this is simply not true."
>
> —FRED BUCY

How can you keep learning?

Stay in Continual Conversation with People

Keep connecting on the heart level. Ask about what has touched their hearts up to now; if their responses are different, then you know they are changing, and you have a new opportunity to learn about what matters to them now.

Look for "Change Indicators"

There are certain times in people's lives when they are most likely to change:

When they *hurt* enough that they *have to*
When they *learn* enough that they *want to*, and
When they *receive* enough that they are *able to*.

Tune into these change indicators, and they will prompt you to recognize that the way you have connected with and helped someone in the past is about to be different, and you need to adjust accordingly.

I need to mention one more thing about this process of learning what matters to people. While it will make you more likeable to people, you must always keep your motives pure, learning about them for their benefit, not yours. Knowing what matters to a person, possessing what I call "the key to their heart," is a great trust. It makes them vulnerable. You must only ever "turn the key" to add value to them, never to manipulate them or serve yourself. If you honor that, you remain trustworthy, and that's one of the most attractive qualities of all.

LISTEN WITH AN OPEN HEART

The most important thing in communication
is to hear what isn't being said.

—PETER DRUCKER

I have a confession to make. While I have always been a people person, and I exhibit what the researchers at Gallop call "WOO," I haven't always been a good listener. In fact, early in my career, I was horrible. My problem was that I thought I knew it all. The only reason I let people talk was that I knew my turn to talk was coming. And I believed if I talked long enough, I could convince anyone of anything.

My wakeup call came when one of my employees had the courage to confront me and tell me what a terrible listener I was. As much as it hurt, I realized she was telling me the truth. I didn't listen to people at work. And in my marriage, I was *little* better. I very much *wanted* to listen to Margaret because of my love for her. However, that didn't stop me from being Mr. Answer Man. I used to win arguments but run over her emotionally. When I finally understood how I was hurting her feelings, I started listening more, not just to her words, but to the feelings behind her words. I learned to listen with an open heart. And our relationship improved.

OPEN YOUR EARS *AND* YOUR HEART

President Woodrow Wilson said, "The ear of the leader must ring with the voices of the people."[1] Every good leader I've ever met was a good listener. Every great leader listened with not only their ears, but also their heart.

If you are a poor listener, as I once was, I want to help you improve. If you are already a good listener, you already are on your way to becoming a better, more charismatic leader. All you need to do is engage your heart to develop greater empathy and understanding so that you can also listen "between the lines" for cues that will tell you how others feel. Either way, here are four tips to help you improve:

1. FOCUS ON THE OTHER PERSON

Herb Cohen, often called the world's best negotiator, said, "Effective listening requires more than hearing the words transmitted. It demands that you find meaning and understanding in what is being said. After all, meanings are not in words, but in people."[2] Many people put their focus on the ideas being communicated, and they almost seem to forget about the person. You can't do that and listen with the heart. You need to keep the person in focus, first and foremost.

I am naturally very impatient, so I must continually fight

> "Meanings are not in words, but in people."
>
> —HERB COHEN

against the tendency to put my agenda first. I think that is often the case with poor listeners. For many years I wrote an *L* in the corner of my legal pad every time I had a conversation with others to remind me to really listen. If you're impatient, slow down and put the person first. Focus on the individual, not just the ideas being expressed.

2. OPEN YOUR MIND AND HEART

Even after you have begun to focus on the person with whom you are conversing, you may still experience many potential barriers to effective listening. Open your mind and heart by removing some of these things that prevent you from listening well:

- **Distractions**—Phone calls, TV, computers, and things of that sort can make good listening nearly impossible.
- **Defensiveness**—If you view complaints or criticism as a personal attack, you may become defensive. If you begin to protect yourself, you will care little about what others say, think, or feel.
- **Closed-mindedness**—When you think you have all the answers, you stop listening. And when you close your mind, you close your ears.

- **Projection**—Automatically attributing your own thoughts and feelings to others prevents you from perceiving how they feel.
- **Assumptions**—When you jump to conclusions, you take away any incentive to listen.
- **Pride**—Thinking we have little to learn from another person is, perhaps, the deadliest of distractions to listening. Being full of yourself leaves little room for input from anyone else.

Obviously, your goal is to remove these barriers to good communication. Whenever possible, put yourself in a good physical environment for listening—away from noise and distractions. And put yourself in a good *mental* environment for listening—set aside your defenses and preconceived notions so that you are *open* to communication.

3. LISTEN PROACTIVELY

There's a difference between listening passively and listening proactively. To listen with your heart, your listening must be active. In his book *It's Your Ship*, Captain Michael Abrashoff explained that people are more likely to speak aggressively than to listen aggressively. When he decided to become an intentional listener, it made a huge difference in him and his crew. He wrote:

It didn't take me long to realize that my young crew was smart, talented, and full of good ideas that frequently came to nothing because no one in charge had ever listened to them. Like most organizations, the Navy seemed to put managers in a transmitting mode, which minimized their receptivity. They were conditioned to promulgate orders from above, not to welcome suggestions from below.

I decided that my job was to listen aggressively and to pick up every good idea the crew had for improving the ship's operation. Some traditionalists might consider this heresy, but it's actually just common sense. After all, the people who do the nuts-and-bolts work on a ship constantly see things that officers don't. It seemed to me only prudent for the captain to work hard at seeing the ship through the crew's eyes. . . . Something happened in me as a result of those interviews. I came to respect my crew enormously. No longer were they nameless bodies at which I barked orders. I realized that they . . . had hopes, dreams, loved ones, and they wanted to believe that what they were doing was important. And they wanted to be treated with respect.[3]

As Abrashoff's attitude changed, his crew transformed, his ship turned around, and the results were astounding. To become a better listener, make your listening *active*.

4. LISTEN TO UNDERSTAND

The fundamental cause of nearly all communication problems is that people don't listen to understand; they listen to reply. David Burns, a medical doctor and professor of psychiatry at the University of Pennsylvania, said: "The biggest mistake you can make in trying to talk convincingly is to put your highest priority on expressing your ideas and feelings. What most people really want is to be listened to, respected, and understood."[4] If you want to connect with people and listen with an open heart, stop focusing on what you think and the response you could make to be right. Listen to understand.

> There's a difference between listening passively and listening proactively. To listen with your heart, your listening must be active.

One of the ironies of becoming a good listener is that listening to others and making them feel understood also has a side benefit. According to Burns, "The moment people see that they are being understood, they become more motivated

> "What most people really want is to be listened to, respected, and understood."
>
> —DAVID BURNS

to understand your point of view."[5] Listening with the heart produces a win-win situation in relationships.

Too often we associate charisma with bold and skilled actions we take: speaking well publicly, performing our job with élan, doing something heroic. While those things can make us stand out, one of the best ways to connect with people and develop rapport with them is to be quiet, pay attention, and listen with our whole being. Try it and see how people respond to you.

8

LEARN EVERYONE'S STORY

Many a man would rather you heard his
story than granted his request.

—PHILLIP STANHOPE, EARL OF CHESTERFIELD

One of the best ways to connect with people is to learn their story. Whenever I have enough time with someone, I ask them to tell me about themselves and give me their story. It's a great way to learn about their journey in life, as well as their interests, hopes, dreams, disappointments, and challenges. Not only that, but it also focuses me entirely on them, which not only gives them the spotlight and makes them feel important, but it also lets them know I care about them. Even on the rare occasions you meet with someone who *doesn't* want to tell their story, you still learn a lot about them. It's a signal that you must proceed more carefully and may need to work to earn greater trust before trying to lead them.

TO APPRECIATE SOMEONE'S STORY, FOLLOW THREE SIMPLE STEPS

Here is some great news about this connecting skill. Anyone can do it. You don't need experience. You don't need to be a good communicator. You don't need to be an extrovert. (In fact, this is one of the most useful connecting skills introverts can employ.) All you need to do is three things:

1. ASK WITH GENUINE INTEREST

When you meet someone new, after the introductions and initial pleasantries, don't hesitate to ask a person about their story. You can do that any number of ways: you can be direct, and ask, "What's your story?" You can ask people to tell you about themselves. You can ask where someone is from or how they got into their field. Use your own style.

If you've never tried this kind of thing before and you worry that it might be awkward the first few times you do it, then practice with people you are unlikely to see again—the driver in a cab, a passenger on a plane, a server in a restaurant. Once you become comfortable asking questions of total strangers, the rest will be easy.

And don't be reluctant to ask again with people you already know and part of whose story you already know. Anytime someone offers a new detail about themselves or states a strong opinion, ask follow-up questions:

- "I haven't heard you mention that before. What happened?"

- "Wow, that's really interesting. I bet there's a story behind that."
- "I didn't know that. Can you tell me more about it?"
- "Why do you feel so strongly about this issue?"

Each time you do this you're opening doors and developing a deeper relationship, which creates greater connection.

2. LISTEN ACTIVELY

I've already told you that I haven't always been a good listener. I've had to work on not only being quiet, but also focusing my attention on others so that I listen actively. Years ago, I came across a list of suggestions for good listening. (I think I clipped it from *Bits and Pieces*.) Here were some of the tips it offered:

- **Look the speaker in the eye.** This communicates that you care.
- **Be attentive.** Don't look at your phone or become distracted.
- **Be respectful.** If you hear something you disagree with, don't roll your eyes or grimace.
- **Don't interrupt.** If you do feel compelled to, say something like, "Go on," or "I see."
- **Repeat back.** Let the speaker know you understand by

saying, "This is what I think I heard. Do I have that right?"

The main idea is to really focus on the other person. The problem many people have is that while the other person speaks, they are thinking more about what they want to say when it's their turn instead of focusing on listening and understanding. When you give people your undivided attention, then you are in a better position to take the next step.

3. REMEMBER THEIR STORY

Some people have a knack for numbers, others for names or faces. But just about everyone has the capacity to remember a story. Why? Stories are how we make sense of the world. They have been recited and sung from memory for thousands of years. Even long stories, such as *The Iliad* and *The Odyssey*—believed to have been created nearly three thousand years ago—were sung for three centuries before being written down. Stories stay with us. Even small children love and remember stories—although they can't always *tell* them in a coherent fashion.

The whole process of connecting with someone through their story can do a lot to communicate your positive feelings toward them and build greater rapport with them. Here's how this works:

- **Requesting** a person's story says, "You could be special."
- **Remembering** a person's story says, "You are special."
- **Reminding** a person of his or her story says, "You are special to me."
- **Repeating** a person's story to others says, "You should be special to them."

If we care about people, really listen to them, and try to remember their stories, we can learn who they are, and we're in a better place to help them, lead them, and make a positive impact on them.

9

EXPRESS HOW MUCH YOU VALUE SOMEONE

Admonish thy friends in secret, praise them openly.

—PUBLILIUS SYRUS

The most fundamental and straightforward way of developing a connection with people is to express how much you value them. A sincere compliment lets a person know how much you value them. That has a great impact when given one-on-one. That impact becomes multiplied by ten when you do it in front of others. A compliment made in the presence of their colleagues tells the team how valuable someone is. A compliment made in hearing of your boss expresses how valuable they are to the organization. And a compliment to someone in the presence of their loved ones has the most value of all because it shows that the one who is important to them is important to you. A private compliment turned public, instantly and dramatically increases in value.

> A compliment to someone in the presence of their loved ones has the most value of all because it shows that the one who is important to them is important to you.

THE VALUE OF VALUING OTHERS

To develop rapport with people and let them know how much you care, value them verbally. Here are reasons why:

COMPLIMENTS MAKE PEOPLE FEEL VALUED

"Everyone has an invisible sign hanging from his neck," said Mary Kay Ash, the founder of Mary Kay Cosmetics. "It says, 'Make Me Feel Important!'" Mary Kay drilled this principle into her sales team. She told them again and again, "Never forget this message when working with people." She knew compliments and affirmation were critical to enjoying success with others.

And by the way, it's one of the reasons she was so successful. With her life savings of $5,000 and the help of her then twenty-year-old son, she launched Mary Kay Cosmetics in 1963. Now millions of independent beauty consultants sell the company's products in nearly forty countries around the world.[1] Mary Kay Cosmetics is one of the most respected direct-sales organizations in the United States and around the world.

Mary Kay, like every other person who wins with people, knew that people want to feel worthwhile. And when you continually keep this in mind, you can't help but give compliments freely.

COMPLIMENTS INCREASE IN VALUE WHEN WE VALUE THE PERSON WHO GIVES THEM

Willard Scott, the late longtime weatherman on NBC's *Today Show*, remembered his radio days when he received his all-time favorite letter from a fan:

Dear Mr. Scott, I think you're the best disk jockey in Washington. You play the best music and have the nicest voice of anyone on the air. Please excuse the crayon; they won't let us have anything sharp in here.[2]

Not all compliments are created equal. Who gives the compliment has a lot to do with how much we prize it.

As commander of a $1 billion warship and a crew of 310, Mike Abrashoff used grassroots leadership to increase retention rates from 28 percent to 100 percent, reduce operating expenditures, and improve readiness. How did he do it? Among other things, he placed supreme importance on public compliments.

"The commanding officer of a ship is authorized to hand out 15 medals a year," he wrote. "I wanted to err on the side of excess, so I passed out 115." Nearly every time a sailor left his ship for another assignment, Captain Abrashoff gave him or her a medal. "Even if they hadn't been star players, they got medals in a public ceremony as long as they had done their best every day. I delivered a short speech describing how much we cherished the recipient's friendship, camaraderie, and hard work. . . . Sometimes the departing sailor's shipmates told funny stories, recalling his or her foibles, trials, and triumphs." But the bottom line was that Abrashoff wanted to make them feel good by complimenting them in front of others.

"There is absolutely no downside to this symbolic gesture," said Abrashoff, "provided it is done sincerely without hype." Captain D. Michael Abrashoff knew how to make his sailors feel worthwhile and valued. No wonder his crew loved him.[3]

COMPLIMENTS AFFIRM PEOPLE AND MAKE THEM STRONG

To affirm is to make firm. An affirmation is a statement of truth you make firm in a person's heart when you utter it. As a result, it cultivates conviction. For example, when you compliment a person's attitude, you reinforce it and make it more consistent. Because you notice it in a positive way, they will be more likely to demonstrate that same attitude again.

Likewise, when you affirm people's dreams, you help their dreams become more real than their doubts. Like the repetition of a weight-lifting regimen, routine compliments build up people's qualities and strengthen their personalities.

"There are high spots in all of our lives," wrote George

Matthew Adams, "and most of them have come about through encouragement from someone else. I don't care how great, how famous or successful a man or woman may be, each hungers for applause. Encouragement is oxygen to the soul. Good work can never be expected from a worker without encouragement. No one can ever have lived without it."

> "Encouragement is oxygen to the soul."
> —GEORGE MATTHEW ADAMS

COMPLIMENTS IN FRONT OF OTHERS ARE THE MOST EFFECTIVE ONES YOU CAN GIVE

Whenever you have the opportunity to praise another person publicly, don't let it slip by. You can do it in the moment, but you can make a huge impact on others when you're intentional and plan to tell others how much you value someone on your team. I try to do this all the time because I know how much it can lift up a person. But sometimes I'm surprised by the impact it can make.

Thirty years ago, Charlie Wetzel came to work with me as my writing partner. I learned quickly that he was a good writer, a hard worker, and an initiative taker. A few months after I hired him, I was doing a lesson to my staff for my tape club (similar to a podcast with fifteen thousand listeners today) on the characteristics of leaders called "Searching for Eagles."

I decided to tell my audience about this young eagle. I had no idea how much it would mean to Charlie. He later told me,

> As you ended the lesson, I had no idea you would say anything about me. You said so many kind and complimentary things about me that it brought tears to my eyes. At that point in my life, I was starved for validation and had rarely been supported in that way. It was overwhelming. Before that moment, I'd never thought of myself as an "eagle." Even to this day, it touches my heart when I think about it.[4]

Since we've been working together, Charlie has helped me write forty-two books. In addition, he has worked to create more than seventy additional supplemental books for me. It's been a highly productive and rewarding friendship and partnership. And Charlie knows how much I value him because I tell him.

If you want to show someone in your life how much you value them—whether it's an employee, a colleague, a client, your spouse, your child, another family member, a friend, or a neighbor—then compliment them sincerely. Do it every chance you get, and if you can, do it in front of others. Few things can break the ice faster in a new relationship or build up an established relationship better than expressing how you value someone.

PART 2

BECOME INVESTED
IN PEOPLE

10

BE QUICK TO HELP OTHERS

After the verb "to love," "to help" is the
most beautiful verb in the world.

—BERTHA VON SUTTNER

My friend Zig Ziglar said, "You can get everything in life you want if you will just help enough other people get what they want."[1] Zig was certainly living proof of that. He helped so many people, and he became a success as a result.

I like helping people. I think it's one of the reasons God put us here on earth. But helping people does more than benefit others. It also helps you win them over. I say that because whenever you are quick to help others, it makes a statement. *You matter to me.* It's like leaving a calling card they will never forget.

BECOME A LEADER WHO HELPS

So how do you become someone who is quick to help others? Follow these guidelines:

MAKE HELPING OTHERS A PRIORITY

We are often so consumed with our own agendas that helping others never becomes important to us. The solution is to make helping others *part* of your agenda—a top priority. Years ago,

I read about something Academy Award–winner Tom Hanks did on the set of *The Green Mile*. It showed how helping others is a priority for him. The film's director, Frank Darabont, reflected on Hanks's commitment to helping rising actor Michael Duncan achieve his best, and the impression it made on him. Darabont said:

> "You can get everything in life you want if you will just help enough other people get what they want."
>
> —ZIG ZIGLAR

Fifteen, twenty years from now, what will I remember [about filming *The Green Mile*]? There was one thing—and I'll never forget this: As we're shooting, [the camera] is on Michael Duncan first, and I'm realizing that I'm getting distracted by Hanks. Hanks is delivering an Academy Award–winning performance, off-camera, for Michael Duncan—to give him every possible thing he needs or can use to deliver the best possible performance. He wanted Michael to do so well. He wanted him to look so good. I'll never forget that.[2]

Tom Hanks, like some other Hollywood actors, could have done the minimum and made it difficult for Duncan. Instead, he was the first to help. It obviously paid off. In 1999,

Michael Clarke Duncan was nominated for an Academy Award in the Best Actor in a Supporting Role category. And Duncan's career took off.

MAKE YOURSELF AWARE OF PEOPLE'S NEEDS

This may sound obvious, but you can't meet a need if you don't know it exists. Each of us must begin by caring about the people around us and looking for what they need. Sometimes that knowledge can come from listening with your heart. Sometimes it comes from just paying attention to what's going on around you. Other times it comes from mentally putting yourself in another person's place.

There is a Jewish legend that says two brothers once shared a field and a mill, each night dividing the grain they had ground together during the day. One brother lived alone; the other was married with a large family.

One day the single brother thought to himself, *It isn't fair that we divide the grain evenly. I have only myself to care for, but my brother has children to feed.* So each night he secretly took some of his flour to his brother's storehouse.

But the married brother considered his brother's situation, and said to himself, It isn't right that we divide the grain evenly, because I have children to provide for me in my old age, but my brother has no one. What will he do when he's old? So every night he secretly took some of his flour and put it in his brother's stores. As a result, both of the brothers found their supply of grain mysteriously replenished each morning.

Then one night they met each other halfway between their two houses. They suddenly realized what the other was doing, and they embraced each other in love. The legend is that God witnessed their meeting and proclaimed, "This is a holy place—a place of love—and here it is that my temple shall be built." The first temple is said to have been constructed on that very site.[3]

BE WILLING TO TAKE A RISK

Sometimes helping another person can be a risky proposition, yet that should not keep us from lending a hand. Ken Sutterfield told a story from the 1936 Olympic Games in Berlin, Germany, that illustrates the impact that can be made by taking such a risk. Coming into the games, American sprinter Jesse Owens had set three world records in one day, including a leap of 26 feet 8–1/4 inches in the running broad jump—a record that would stand for twenty-five years. However, Owens faced great pressure during the games. Hitler and his fellow Nazis wanted to use the competition to display presumed Aryan superiority, and Owens, a Black man, could sense the hostility toward him.

As Owens tried to qualify for the finals during the games, he became rattled as he saw a tall, blue-eyed, blond German taking practice jumps in the 26-foot range. On his first jump, Owens leaped from several inches beyond the takeoff board. Then he fouled on the second attempt. He was allowed only one more attempt. If he missed it, he would be eliminated.

The tall German approached Owens and introduced himself. His name was Luz Long. As the Nazis watched, Long encouraged Owens and offered him some advice: since the qualifying distance was only 23 feet 5 1/2 inches, Long suggested that Owens make a mark several inches before the takeoff board to make sure he didn't foul. Owens qualified on his third jump. In the finals, he set an Olympic record and earned one of his four gold medals. And who was the first person to congratulate Owens? Luz Long!

Owens never forgot the risk Long took and encouraging help he had given him, though he never saw Long again. "You could melt down all the medals and cups I have," Owens wrote, "and they wouldn't be plating on the 24-carat friendship I felt for Luz Long."[4]

FOLLOW THROUGH NO MATTER WHAT

Philanthropist Andrew Carnegie was approached for financial support by members of the New York Philharmonic Society, one of Carnegie's favorite charities. He was about to write a check to wipe out the Society's entire deficit when suddenly he stopped. "Surely, there must be other rich, generous music lovers in this town who could help out," he said. "Why don't you raise half this amount, and come back to me for the other half," said the great philanthropist.

The next day, the treasurer came back and told Carnegie that he had raised $30,000 and would like now to get Carnegie's check. The patron of the arts was immensely pleased at this show of enterprise and immediately handed it over. But he was curious. "Who, may I ask, contributed the other half?"

"Mrs. Carnegie," came the reply.

Sometimes when we help others, we discover their need wasn't as great as we expected. Follow through anyway. It's never wrong to be generous, and don't begrudge what you've given.

When you help someone who doesn't know you, it can win them over. When you help people with whom you already have a connection, it endears you to them even more. And when you help others whose attitude toward you isn't positive, they reevaluate their assessment of you and let their guard down. Being quick to help is a great way to win with people.

INVITE PEOPLE TO
JOIN YOUR TEAM

The greatest compliment that was ever paid me was when
one asked me what I thought, and attended to my answer.

—HENRY DAVID THOREAU

The day that I realized I could no longer do everything myself was a major step in my development as a person and a leader. I've always had vision, plenty of ideas, and vast amounts of energy. But when the vision gets bigger than you, you really only have two choices: give up on the vision or get help. I chose the latter.

I made this breakthrough discovery in 1974. I was facing a major building project, and I needed to raise more than a million dollars. It was the first time I understood how far over my head I truly was in leadership. That's when I realized that if I was ever to achieve something great, I needed to turn the dream from *me* to *we*. As I thought about this, I started to get an idea. What if I could paint the picture of the vision I saw in words and create an invitation I could give to others to join me? It took me many hours over the course of a week, and this was the result:

> When the vision gets bigger than you, you really only have two choices: give up on the vision or get help.

I HAVE A DREAM

History tells us that in every age there comes a time when leaders must come forth to meet the needs of the hour. Therefore, there is no potential leader who does not have an opportunity to better mankind. Those around him also have the same privilege. Fortunately, I believe that God has surrounded me with those who will accept the challenge of this hour.

My dream allows me to . . .

- Give up at any moment all that I am in order to receive all that I can become.
- Sense the invisible so I can do the impossible.
- Trust God's resources since the dream is bigger than all my abilities and acquaintances.
- Continue when discouraged, for where there is no faith in the future, there is no power in the present.
- Attract winners, because big dreams draw big people.
- See my people and myself in the future. Our dream is the promise of what we shall one day be.

Yes, I have a dream. It is greater than any of my gifts. It is as large as the world, but it begins with one. Won't you join me?

—JOHN MAXWELL

I had these words beautifully printed on cards, and as I asked people to help me, I gave them out. As a result, hundreds of people came along side me and became part of the team. And together, we accomplished the vision.

MAKE THE INVITATION

No matter how successful you are, no matter how important or accomplished, you *do* need people. That's why you need to let them know that you cannot win without them. President Woodrow Wilson said, "We should not only use all the brains we have—but all that we can borrow."[1] Why stop with just their brains? Enlist people's hands and hearts too! Another president, Lyndon Johnson, was right when he said, "There are no problems we cannot solve together, and very few that we can solve by ourselves."[2]

Asking others for their help is a great way to connect with them. Here's why:

PEOPLE NEED TO BE NEEDED

Have you ever stopped to ask someone for directions? Nearly every time, people stop whatever they are doing and help if they can—even if it means crossing the street or walking you to your destination. They may even repeat the directions a couple of times to make sure you get it. Why? Because whenever a person feels that he or she knows something you don't, it makes that person feel good. Everyone likes to be an expert, even if it's for a moment. It gives them a great sense of superiority and of accomplishment when they help. That translates into an increased sense of self-worth. And it all stems from the universal need to be needed.

PEOPLE NEED TO KNOW THEY NEED OTHERS

"It marks a big step in your development when you come to realize that other people can help you do a better job than you could do alone," said steel magnate and philanthropist Andrew Carnegie. Sadly, many people never achieve that level of maturity or insight. Some people still want to believe that they can achieve greatness alone.

Every individual's fate is tied to that of many others. We cannot be like the shipwrecked man who sits at one end of a lifeboat doing nothing while everyone at the other end bails furiously, and says, "Thank God that hole isn't in *my* end of the boat!" We all need people, and if we don't know it, we're in trouble.

PEOPLE NEED TO KNOW THEY ARE NEEDED

Cartoonist Charles Schulz often captured the longings of the human heart in his comic strip *Peanuts*. He really understood the needs of people. In one of his creations, Lucy asks Charlie Brown to help with her homework. "I'll be eternally grateful," she promises.

"Fair enough. I've never had anyone be eternally grateful before," replies Charlie. "Just subtract 4 from 10 to get how many apples the farmer had left."

Lucy says, "That's it? That's it? I have to be eternally grateful for that? I was robbed! I can't be eternally grateful for this, it was too easy!"

With a look of discouragement, Charlie replies, "Well, whatever you think is fair."

"How about if I just say 'thanks, Bro'?" replies Lucy.

As Charlie leaves to go outside, he meets Linus, who asks, "Where've you been, Charlie Brown?"

"Helping Lucy with her homework."

"Did she appreciate it?" Linus asks.

Charlie responds, "At greatly reduced prices."[3]

If you've ever felt like Charlie Brown, you're not alone. Every human being longs for a life of significance. We all need to know we are needed and that what we offer to others is of value.

PEOPLE NEED TO KNOW THEY HELPED

Whenever someone tells me how valuable the people on my team are to them, I encourage him to tell the individuals who were so helpful. Why? Because people need to know that they helped someone. "Good leaders make people feel that they're at the very heart of things, not at the periphery," said author and leadership expert Warren Bennis. "Everyone feels that he or she makes a difference to the success of the organization. When that happens people feel centered and that gives their work meaning."[4]

Walter Shipley, who was chairman and CEO of Chase Manhattan Bank, one said, "We have 68,000 employees. With a company this size, I'm not 'running the business.' . . . My job is to create the environment that enables people to leverage each other beyond their own individual capabilities. . . . I get credit for providing the leadership that got us there. But our people did it."[5] Shipley understood what all successful leaders know: people need to know that they made an important contribution to reaching the goal.

> "Good leaders make people feel that they're at the very heart of things, not at the periphery."
>
> —WARREN BENNIS

It's not a sign of weakness to let others know you value them. Inviting people to become part of your team is a sign of security and strength. When you're honest about your need for help, specific with others about the value they add, and inclusive of others as you build a team to do something bigger than you are, everybody wins.

ENCOURAGE THE DREAMS OF OTHERS

Keep away from people who try to belittle your ambitions. Small people always do that, but the really great make you feel that you, too, can become great.

—MARK TWAIN

I consider it a great privilege when anyone shares their dreams with me. It shows a great deal of courage and trust. And at that moment, I'm conscious that I have great power to help them or harm them. That's no small matter. A wrong word can crush a person's dream; the right word can inspire them to pursue it.

THE POWER OF A DREAM

If someone thinks enough of you to tell you about their dreams, take care. Even if you privately have doubts about the viability of their dream, don't doubt them or discourage them. Instead, encourage them and keep these things in mind:

DREAMS ARE FRAGILE

Actress Candice Bergen commented, "Dreams are, by definition, cursed with short lifespans."[1] I suspect she said that because there are people who don't like to see others pursuing their dreams. It reminds them of how far they are from living their own dreams. As a result, they try to knock down anyone who is shooting for the stars. By trying to talk others out of their dreams, critical people excuse themselves for staying in their comfort zone. Never allow yourself to become a dream killer. Instead, become a dream encourager.

> "Dreams are, by definition, cursed with short lifespans."
> —CANDICE BERGEN

LOSING A DREAM IS A GREAT LOSS

Have you given up one of your dreams? Have you buried a hope that once looked bright and gave you energy? If so, what did it do to you? Norman Cousins, former editor of the *Saturday Review* and adjunct professor of psychiatry at UCLA, believed, "Death is not the greatest loss in life. The greatest loss is what dies inside of us while we live."

Our dreams keep us alive. Benjamin Franklin observed, "Most men die from the neck up at age twenty-five because they stop dreaming."[2] That's why it's so important that you help keep others' dreams alive. By doing so, you can literally help them live. Encouraging another person's dream can nurture their soul.

> "Death is not the greatest loss in life. The greatest loss is what dies inside of us while we live."
> —NORMAN COUSINS

ENCOURAGING OTHERS TO PURSUE A DREAM IS A WONDERFUL GIFT

Because dreams are at the center of our souls, we must do everything in our power to help turn dreams into reality. That is one of the greatest gifts we can ever give others. How can you do it? Follow these six steps:

1. **Ask them to share their dream with you.** Everyone has a dream, but few people are asked about it.

2. **Affirm the person as well as the dream.** Let the person know that you not only value their dream but that you also recognize traits in that individual that can help them achieve it.

3. **Ask about the challenges they must overcome to reach their dream.** Few people ask others about their dreams; even fewer try to find out what kinds of hurdles the person must jump to pursue them.

4. **Offer your assistance.** No one achieves a worthwhile dream alone. You'll be amazed by how people light up when you offer to help them achieve their dream.

5. **Revisit their dream with them on a consistent basis.** If you really want to help others with their dreams, don't make it a one-time activity you mark off your list. Check in with them to see how they're doing and to lend assistance.

6. **Remind yourself daily to be a dream booster, not dream buster.** Everyone has a dream, and everyone needs encouragement. Set your mental radar to pick up on others' dreams and help them along.

You will be amazed by the positive impact you can have on others by encouraging them to pursue their dreams.

PEOPLE LIVE UP TO THEIR DREAMS WHEN GIVEN A CHANCE TO FULFILL THEM

Scott Adams, creator of the popular *Dilbert* cartoon, told this story about his beginnings as a cartoonist:

When I was trying to become a syndicated cartoonist, I sent my portfolio to one cartoon editor after another—and received one rejection after another. One editor even called and suggested that I take art classes. Then Sarah Gillespie, an editor at United Media and one of the real experts in the field, called to offer me a contract. At first, I didn't believe her. I asked if I'd have to change my style, get a partner—or learn how to draw. But she believed I was already good enough to be a nationally syndicated cartoonist.

Her confidence in me completely changed my frame of reference: it altered how I thought about my own abilities. This may sound bizarre, but from the minute I got off the phone with her, I could draw better. You can see a marked improvement in the quality of the cartoons I drew after that conversation.[3]

Editor Sarah Gillespie gave Adams a chance to live out his dream, but because so many people had tried to discourage him, he was almost afraid to say yes. But because of Gillespie's encouragement—and the opportunity she gave him—*Dilbert* became one of the most popular cartoons in the nation.

There is no telling what might happen if you were to begin encouraging the dreams of the people around you. When you come to the end of your life, wouldn't you love to be the person about whom others said, "I succeeded because this person believed in me when nobody else did"? Start encouraging others. The more you do, the more they will share their dreams with you. And the greater the chance you will get to watch them bloom.

13

SHARE THE CREDIT
WITH OTHERS

If each of us were to confess his most secret
desire, the one that inspires all his plans, all his
actions, he would say: "I want to be praised."

—E. M. CIORAN

When I wrote my first book in 1979, I never dreamed anything I wrote would become a bestseller. But in 1998, my book *The 21 Laws of Leadership* made it onto the *New York Times*. Five years later in July of 2003, the book hit another milestone I never thought possible. It sold one million copies. To celebrate that accomplishment and to honor me, Thomas Nelson, who published the book, hosted a celebratory banquet in Orlando for about 120 people from their company and mine. They gave me some beautiful gifts that night, including a set of gold cuff links with the number 21 on them and a crystal eagle.

My favorite moment that night was when I got to thank all the people who made that book possible. Victor Oliver had come up with the original concept for the book and provided the title. Dan Reiland, Tim Elmore, and Charlie Wetzel helped me hone the laws, and Charlie worked as my writing partner to finish the book. Ron Land from Thomas Nelson and the team from my company put together the tour that launched the book. And publisher Mike Hyatt led the entire sales and marketing staff who got into bookstores across the country. It was a true team effort.

Making a book successful and getting it into the hands of people it can help is always a team effort, though not all authors see it that way. Everybody involved in the process has a part to play. I wanted them to know that they had made it all possible. Rarely do we get an opportunity to say thank you enough to the people who help us.

HOW TO GIVE OTHERS CREDIT

Passing the credit on to others is one of the easiest ways to connect with people and make yourself more attractive to them as a leader. If that's what you desire, take these suggestions to heart:

CHECK YOUR EGO AT THE DOOR

The number one reason people don't pass along credit to others is that they think it will somehow hurt them or lesson their value. Many leaders are so insecure that they constantly feed their egos to compensate for it. But you simply cannot be an authentic, humble leader unless you can set your ego aside.

Have you ever heard the saying "An egotist is not a person

who thinks too much of himself; it's someone who thinks too little of other people"? If you want to give others credit, put your focus on them, not yourself. Ask yourself: What do they need? How will giving them credit make them feel? How will it enhance their performance? How will it motivate them to reach their potential? If you highlight their contributions, it makes them *and* you look good.

> "An egotist is not a person who thinks too much of himself; it's someone who thinks too little of other people."

PASS ON THE CREDIT AT YOUR FIRST OPPORTUNITY

I love what H. Ross Perot once said about passing on credit: "Reward employees while the sweat's still on their brow."[1] Isn't it true that one of the very best times to give credit to others is when the amount of work they did and sacrifices they made are still fresh in their minds? Why wait? You may have heard management expert Ken Blanchard's teaching that you should catch people while they're doing something good. What a great idea! The sooner you give credit to someone else, the bigger the payoff.

In 2003, when I met with UCLA basketball coach John Wooden for the first time, he told me how he would often teach his players who scored to give a smile, wink, or nod to the player who gave them a good pass. "What if he's not looking?" asked a team member. Wooden replied, "I guarantee he'll look." Everyone enjoys having his contribution acknowledged.

GIVE CREDIT PUBLICLY

You've already read the chapter where I encouraged to express people's values to others, but it bears repeating. When you give credit to others in front of their peers and loved ones, the value of it multiplies greatly. Private recognition is valuable. Public recognition is off the charts. Former New York Yankees player and manager Billy Martin observed, "There's nothing greater in the world than when somebody on the team does something good and everybody gathers around to pat him on the back."[2] By giving credit in a crowd, you can help to create the kind of environment Martin described.

PUT IT IN PRINT

When you give people credit verbally, you uplift them for a moment. When you take the time to put it in writing, you have the potential to lift them up for a lifetime. People put plaques on their walls as reminders of their achievements. They save and cherish letters containing recognition and praise for things they've done. Deep down, everyone wants to make a difference, and some days, everyone needs some encouragement.

I have a file in my office with letters and notes that have special significance for me. Every now and then, I'll pull out the file and read some of the things people I respect have written to me. It allows me to relive that moment of encouragement. It's said that even President Abraham Lincoln used to carry in his pocket a newspaper clipping extolling his accomplishments as president. He was one of the finest leaders in our nation's history, yet he desired something to keep his spirits up.

Please don't underestimate the impact that an article, a public notice, or a personal note can make. What takes you only a few minutes to write may be something that inspires another person for decades.

SAY IT ONLY IF YOU MEAN IT

I love this old joke: As an old man lay dying, his wife of many years sat close by his bed. He opened his eyes and saw her. "There you are, Agnes," he said, "at my side again."

"Yes, dear," she replied.

"Looking back," the old man said, "I remember all the times you were by my side. You were there when I got my draft notice and had to go off to fight in the war. You were with me when our first house burned to the ground. When I had the accident that destroyed our car, you were there. And you were at my side when my business went bankrupt and we lost every cent we had."

"Yes, dear," his wife said.

The old man sighed.

"I tell you, Agnes," he said, "you've been a real jinx."

It may seem obvious, but I want to go ahead and say it anyway so that I'm not misunderstood. You should never say something you don't believe just to lift up someone. If you're not sincere, you don't make people feel good; you make them feel they're being schmoozed. When you pass credit on to others, you need to do it from the heart.

The members of a team always know who did most of the heavy lifting when they worked together on something, and they feel it's only right for them to be acknowledged for their contribution. Any leader who takes too much credit loses the respect of their team. But leaders who are humble and put others in the spotlight are respected and admired. Those are the kind of leaders people are happy to work with and for.

CREATE SPECIAL
MOMENTS FOR OTHERS

Memory is the treasury and guardian of all things.

—CICERO

Few things bond people together like a shared memory. Soldiers who battle together, teammates who win a championship, and working teams that hit their goals share a connection that never goes away. Married couples who experience rough times can often look back on their earlier experiences together to keep them going. Families bond when they rough it on camping trips or share adventures on vacation, which they later love recounting.

Some memories come as the result of circumstances, but many can be proactively created by a leader. Author Lewis Carroll wrote, "It's a poor sort of memory that only works backward."[1] What does that mean to you and me? The richest memories are often those we plan and intentionally create.

CHARACTERISTICS OF A MEMORY MAKER

I have become very intentional about creating memories for people, from planning impactful trips with our grandchildren to asking questions at dinner leading to memorable conversations to organizing once-in-a-lifetime events for donors to my leadership foundation. Perhaps I started doing this because I was a fun-loving kid who reveled in the memories my parents first created for our family. I think it actually gives me more joy than it gives to the recipients. When you give someone a great memory, it's something they have forever.

If you want to create memorable moments for others, here are some qualities I recommend you cultivate:

INITIATIVE—MAKE SOMETHING HAPPEN

Memories don't find us—we find them. Even better, if we are intentional, we *make* memories. If you mention the word *chariot* to my friends Dan and Patti Reiland along with Tim and Pam Elmore, I can tell you exactly what will come to mind—a crisp autumn day in New York City when we did something that still makes us laugh. After lunch at Tavern on the Green, I hired three "bicycle chariots" with peddling drivers to take each couple on a race through Manhattan to Macy's. It was up to each couple to motivate their driver to win (using whatever incentives they wanted). The race was neck-and-neck the entire way, and we laughed the whole time.

We still laugh when we think about it or look at the

photos we took that day. But it never would have happened if we hadn't initiated it.

TIME—SET ASIDE TIME TO MAKE SOMETHING HAPPEN

For years parents have debated the issue of quality time versus quantity of time. As a father and grandfather, I have discovered that it takes quantity time to *find* quality time. If you don't carve out the time, you can't create the memory.

Haven't you found that the majority of your most meaningful memories are with the people you spend the most time with? I know that's true for me. If you want to make memories with your family, spend more time with them. If you want to create memories with your employees, come out of your office and do things with them. You simply can't make memories with people if you don't take time to be with them.

PLANNING—PLAN FOR SOMETHING TO HAPPEN

Most people don't lead their lives—they accept their lives. They wait for memorable experiences to happen to them, never giving a thought to planning an experience that will make a memory for themselves and others.

One of the most extravagant memories I ever planned was with Margaret, my wife, for our twenty-fifth wedding anniversary. We decided to share it with thirty of our closest friends. We chartered a yacht and picked everyone up in San Diego Bay. Once on board, we had a delectable meal and then surprised the group by having Frankie Valens entertain us with some of his trademark songs like "Sixteen Candles." Our friends loved it. But the most memorable highlight of the evening was created when Margaret and I said a few words about each person and why that person held such a special place in our hearts. That night is not only a great memory for Margaret and me, but it is a great memory for the people who attended too.

> Most people don't lead their lives— they accept their lives.

CREATIVITY—FIND A WAY TO MAKE SOMETHING HAPPEN

What do you do when you find yourself at an event where you expect to share a memory, but nothing seems to happen? Get creative! I've been asked over and over to tell the story of the Holiday Bowl I attended in San Diego with friends many years ago. The game was so dull that I ended up buying newspapers for everyone in my section of the stadium so that we would have something to do. Seeing what I'd done, another person in the stands decided not to be outdone and bought one hundred bags of peanuts, which he distributed to everybody in the section. The two of us got a standing ovation, and soon the camera crews were more focused on us than the game. I don't remember the score or much about the game, but it's a night I'll never forget. Neither will the buddies who attended the game with me.

SHARED EXPERIENCES—MAKE SOMETHING HAPPEN TOGETHER

Memories compound when they are experienced with someone you love. Years ago, our family went to Jasper Park in Canada for a vacation. While we were there, I took my children, Elizabeth and Joel Porter, fishing. On our way back to our cabin, we called Margaret to let her know we were coming home, and she asked the kids how they did.

> **Memories compound when they are experienced with someone you love.**

"We caught eight trout," Joel said. He was acting low-key about it, but I could tell he was proud. As we drove back, we talked about how great it was going to be to have a dinner of trout we had just pulled from a cold mountain stream. When we arrived, we carried the trout into the kitchen, and there on the counter we saw four steaks ready to be cooked.

"What gives?" Joel asked his mother. "We caught eight trout! And we're looking forward to a trout dinner."

Margaret started to laugh. "I thought you said *a* trout, so I went out and bought steaks." Then I started laughing, and

Elizabeth did too. Finally, with a gleam in his eye, Joel said, "Mom's not too good with numbers, is she?"

That happened with our kids when they were eleven and thirteen years old. Every time we've had a cookout since then, the kids have told the trout story. Even now that both of them are married and have kids of their own, they still love to say, "Mom's not too good with numbers." It makes all of us laugh.

MEMENTOS—SHOW THAT SOMETHING HAPPENED

"Almost anything you do today will be forgotten in just a few weeks," said author and research scientist John McCrone. "The ability to retrieve a memory decreases exponentially . . . unless boosted by artificial aids such as diaries and photographs."[2]

I love to keep memories alive by keeping some kind of memento. It takes me right back to when it happened. Do you like that as well? Do you keep pictures or souvenirs on your desk where you can see them? Do you carry photos of people you love in your wallet? Do you have a trophy, plaque, game ball, or other award on a shelf where you and others can see it? We all have things we love—not because they have any material value but because they remind us of places we've been or things we've done with people we care about. When you help create a memory for others, try to give them something to remember it by.

RELIVE THE MEMORY—TALK ABOUT WHAT HAPPENED

The most important part of creating a memory is reliving it. It is the payoff. Many times when I travel with others, at the end of our trip I ask them to share a favorite memory. It often leads to rich conversations. Or I write a note to someone soon afterward to share my own favorite memory. It creates a connection that bonds us together and makes both of us feel great.

I cannot emphasize enough what creating memories does for the people you influence and for you as a leader. Leaders who go out of their way to know their people and what they value, tailor ways to create memories they'll love, take the time to do the groundwork, and spend the money to make it happen, have a special place in the hearts of the people they lead. Whether you create memories for your spouse, kids, friends, employees, or colleagues, you will become a leader who makes a positive impression and wins their hearts.

SHARE INFORMATION WITH OTHERS

Conceal not your secret from your friend,

or you deserve to lose him.

—PORTUGUESE PROVERB

A Sicilian proverb says, "Only the spoon knows what is stirring in the pot." When you allow another person to know what is stirring within you, giving them a "taste" of a plan or idea, you instantly make a meaningful connection with them. Who doesn't want to know what's going on in the mind of someone they care about? Or learn from their leader what important work their team is trying to accomplish?

In 1996, Margaret and I decided to move our company from San Diego to the Atlanta area. At that time, we employed consultants who flew to help clients all across the country, and living in San Diego made travel very difficult for them. The majority of our clients were located east of the Mississippi River, and our consultants typically lost a day traveling to them. I also traveled extensively as a speaker, and my assistant Linda Eggers looked at my travel schedule from the previous year and estimated that I spent thirty days just making connections. That's what caused us to move the company to an airline hub location.

Before we announced the move publicly, I met individually with key staff to tell them about the move and to invite them to move with us. For some people, that was a big deal. One of those people was Charlie Wetzel. Later, he said that my asking him to come with me made a deep impression. He later said,

> John, our conversation lasted for probably no more than five minutes, but what it communicated to me changed my life. I had worked hard, we'd already written five or six books together, and you were always lavish with your praise. But I had no idea you valued me as much as you did. Sharing that information with me showed me how important I was to you and your vision, and it changed the way I saw myself.[1]

As I've already mentioned, Charlie and I have worked together for thirty years. It is and continues to be a fantastic partnership.

GIVE OTHERS THE INSIDE TRACK

Any time you let people in on something impactful, it makes quite an impression. But you can make sharing information part of your everyday life using everyday things. People especially love being told secrets or being given the inside track. If you're telling someone something you haven't shared before, why not tell them so? That makes him feel special.

Sharing information with someone is really a matter of two things: reading the context of a situation and desiring to build up the other person. If you keep those two things in mind, you can learn this skill and connect with people. As you try it out, keep these three things in mind:

1. SHARE INFORMATION VITAL TO PEOPLE'S SUCCESS

Two experienced deep-sea fishermen decided to try ice fishing for the first time. They each chopped holes in the ice, put worms on their hooks, dropped their lines into the water, and waited. After three hours, they had caught nothing.

As they sat, they watched a boy come along and cut a hole in the ice midway between them. He put a worm on his hook, dropped his line into the water, and almost instantly he caught a fish. The boy repeated the process and quickly had a catch of more than a dozen fish. The two other fishermen watched and were flabbergasted.

Finally, one of the men approached the boy and said, "Young man, we've been here for more than three hours and haven't caught a single fish. You've caught at least a dozen in just a few minutes. What's your secret?"

The boy mumbled an answer, but the man didn't catch

a word of it. Then he noticed a large bulge in the boy's left cheek. "Please, could you take the bubble gum out of your mouth so I can understand what you're saying?" the man said.

The boy cupped his hands, spat it out, and said, "It's not bubble gum; it's my secret. You've got to keep the worms warm."

The most important information a leader can share is the knowledge his team members need to be successful. Too many leaders hold back information their people need either because they don't truly understand how much the information could help them or because they hang onto knowledge because it makes them feel more powerful. Don't fall into those traps. Share everything you can to make another person's job or life easier.

2. SHARE WITH THE GOAL OF MAKING PEOPLE FEEL SPECIAL

Letting people in on something always boosts their egos. If you can let someone in on a secret, that usually builds a connection. The secret doesn't have to be dramatic to have a positive effect. For example, when I play golf, I usually carry a laminated card with me that contains tips given to me by golf pro Scott Szymoniak. Occasionally if a friend in the group is not playing well, I'll pull him aside and say, "I want to share a secret with you that has really helped my golf game." Then I'll pull out the card and show him the six things a golfer must know and do. And I'll let him know that it's my personal golf plan that I don't share with everybody.

How does it make you feel when you know that you're the first person being told something? I know it makes me feel special. That's one of the reasons my wife, Margaret, and I have practiced saving news to tell each other first when we see each other at the end of the day or after a trip apart. It's hard for me to hold onto that information and not tell others, but it's important to me because of the positive effect on mine and Margaret's relationship. These conversations are often our favorite moments together every day.

3. SHARE INFORMATION TO INCLUDE OTHERS IN YOUR JOURNEY

The bottom line on sharing information with others is that it is an act of inclusion. It invites others into your life, into your experience. It includes them in your success. When I speak to an audience—whether it's a roundtable of executives or an arena full of people—I intentionally use inclusive language. I let people in on my personal journey. And when I'm revealing something I've not previously said publicly, I let them know that I'm doing so. It communicates to people that I care about them and want to help them.

> The bottom line on sharing a secret with others is that it is an act of inclusion.

How naturally inclusive are you? Are you an open book, sharing information freely with most people? Or are you naturally private, tending to keep information to yourself? To be a better leader and a more charismatic person, you need to open up. You need to go out of your way to include others and share what you know. It will empower the people you lead, make them feel included, and inspire them to do better work.

16

SPEAK INTO PEOPLE'S LIVES

Treat a man as he appears to be and you make him worse.
But treat a man as if he already were what he potentially
could be, and you make him what he should be.

—GOETHE

One of the best ways to inspire others and make them feel good about themselves is to show them who they could be by speaking into their lives. Years ago, a manager for the New York Yankees wanted his rookie players to know what a privilege it was to play for the team. He used to tell them, "Boys, it's an honor just to put on the New York pinstripes. So when you put them on, play like world champions. Play like Yankees. Play proud."

When you give someone a reputation to uphold, you speak into a person's life, you encourage them to be their best selves. By speaking to their potential, you help them to "play proud," as the Yankees do. Why is that important? Because people will go farther than they thought they could when someone they respect tells them they can.

HOW TO INVEST IN PEOPLE VERBALLY

If you desire to lift people up by speaking into their lives, here are suggestions about how to get started:

HAVE A HIGH OPINION OF THEM

The opinions you have of people in your life affect them profoundly. Dr. J. Sterling Livingston, formerly of the Harvard Business School and founder of the Sterling Institute management consulting firm, observed, "People perform consistently as they perceive you expect them to perform."[1]

One of the ways to express your high opinion of them is to give them a reputation to uphold. Speak of them as you know they could be. A reputation is something that many people spend their entire lives trying to live down or live up to. So why not help others up instead of pushing them down? All people possess both value and potential. You can find those things if you look for them.

BACK UP YOUR HIGH OPINION WITH ACTION

When you back up your belief in people with action, their self-doubt begins to evaporate. It's one thing to tell your teenager that you believe he's a good driver; it's another to let him have the keys to your car for the evening. Likewise, if you want a new manager to rise to the high opinion you've expressed about them, then give them significant responsibility. Nothing gives people confidence like seeing someone they respect put their money where their mouth is. Not only does it empower them emotionally, but it also resources their drive toward success.

LOOK BEYOND THEIR PAST AND PRESENT AN EXPECTATION FOR THE FUTURE

Old negative labels can block a person's growth and progress. Perhaps that's why the rites of passage in many cultures include giving a new title or name to the person being honored. Rather than looking to a person's past, they are focused on their potential future.

As a leader, focus more on the person's potential than their past. See who they can be, and speak into that to inspire them to become their best selves. Harry Hopman, one of the finest tennis captains and coaches in Australia's history and a member of the International Tennis Hall of Fame, at one time built the Australian team to the point that it dominated the tennis world. How did he do it? By emphasizing what he called "coaching by affirmation." For example, he had a slow player whom he nicknamed "Rocket." Another player who was not known for his strength or constitution he called "Muscles." And it certainly gave them a boost. Rocket Rod Laver and Ken "Muscles" Rosewall became champions in the tennis world.

PUT YOUR ENCOURAGEMENT INTO WRITING

French journalist Emile De Girardin said, "The power of words is immense. A well-chosen word has often sufficed to stop a flying army, to change defeat into victory, and to save an empire." I'm a firm believer in the power of written notes of encouragement. A kind word given from the heart is always well received. In his book *The Power of Encouragement*, my friend David Jeremiah wrote, "Written encouragement comes directly from the heart, uninterrupted and uninhibited. That's why it's so powerful."[2] Haven't you known that to be true?

For years I have made it a practice to write personal notes to others. I often forget what I have written, but occasionally someone who has received a note from me will show it to me and tell me what an encouragement it was. It is in those moments that I am reminded of the sustained and repeated encouragement people receive from the written word.

> "Written encouragement comes directly from the heart, uninterrupted and uninhibited. That's why it's so powerful."
>
> —DAVID JEREMIAH

You never can tell when something you write to others will light them up in down times or sustain them when life gets difficult. In the first *Chicken Soup for the Soul* book, teacher Sister Helen Mrosla recounted how a spur-of-the-moment assignment in class became a source of encouragement for her students. On a day when her junior high math students were especially ornery, she asked them to write down what they liked about each of their fellow students. She then compiled the results over the weekend and handed out the lists on the following Monday.

Years later when one of those students, Mark, was killed in Vietnam, she and some of those former students got together for the funeral. Afterward, Mark's father told the group, "They found this on Mark when he was killed," and he showed them a folded, refolded, and taped paper—the one he had received years before from his teacher. Right after that, Charlie, one of Mark's classmates, said, "I keep my list in my desk drawer." Chuck's wife said, "Chuck put his in our wedding album." "I have mine, too," Marilyn said, "in my diary."

Standing there, Vicky reached into her pocketbook and brought out her frazzled list, showing it to her teacher and former classmates. Each person cherished the kind words of encouragement they had received. That's the power of a few kind words.[3]

Few things can compare to the charisma-giving effect of speaking into the lives of others. A great example of that could be found in the life of former British Prime Minister Winston Churchill. During the worst part of World War II, Churchill said of the people in his nation:

> We shall not flag or fail . . . We shall fight in France, we shall fight in the seas and oceans, we shall fight with growing confidence and growing strength in the air, we shall defend our island, whatever the cost

may be, we shall fight on the beaches, we shall fight on the landing grounds, we shall fight in the fields and in the streets, we shall fight in the hills; we shall never surrender . . .[4]

Churchill was not a physically imposing person. He was short and heavy. His voice was not particularly impressive or authoritative. His expression was often serious, and his demeanor was often cranky. Yet, he exuded charisma. Why? He spoke into the lives of an entire nation when it faced a threat against its existence. He inspired, challenged, and motivated people to stay calm and carry on against the Nazis. They loved him for it, and they rose to meet his expectations.

If you want people to admire, respect, and follow you, speak into their lives and bring out their best, not for your sake but for theirs. Not only will they be inspired to achieve more than they thought possible, but they will also be grateful to you for challenging them.

BUILD BRIDGES FOR OTHERS

You have not lived today until you have done
something for someone who can never repay you.

—JOHN BUNYAN

Ambassador and poet Henry Van Dyke observed, "There is a loftier ambition than merely to stand high in the world. It is to stoop down and lift mankind a little higher."[1] What a great perspective! I like to think of this as building bridges for others. When you build a bridge, you make it possible for people to go places and do things they would otherwise never be able to experience.

> "There is a loftier ambition than merely to stand high in the world. It is to stoop down and lift mankind a little higher."
>
> —HENRY VAN DYKE

HOW TO BECOME A BRIDGE-BUILDING LEADER

Doing for others what they can't do for themselves is really a matter of attitude. I believe that whatever I've been given should be shared with others. And because I have an abundance mind-set, I never worry about running out myself. The more I give away, the more I seem to receive so that I can give it away.

No matter how much or how little you think you have, you have the ability to build bridges and do for others what they cannot do for themselves. Exactly how you do that will depend on your unique gifts, resources, and history. However, you can approach the task by thinking in terms of four areas:

1. INTRODUCE OTHERS TO PEOPLE THEY WOULDN'T KNOW ON THEIR OWN

My dad, Melvin Maxwell, did many incredible things for me when I was growing up. One of the things that impacted me most was his introducing me to great leaders. As a teenager, I met Norman Vincent Peale, E. Stanley Jones, and other great people of faith. And because I had declared my intention to go into the ministry, my father asked these great preachers to pray for me. I can't express in words what that did for me.

Today, I am often in a position to do for others what my father did for me. I love introducing young people to my heroes. I enjoy helping people make connections with other business leaders. Many times when I meet someone, they'll say something and it just hits me: *I need to introduce this person to so-and-so.* That can mean walking somebody across the room, making a phone call on their behalf, or arranging a meeting.

Several years ago, I was talking to Anne Beiler, the founder of Auntie Anne's pretzel company, and she mentioned in passing that Chick-fil-A's founder, Truett Cathy, was one of her heroes. Since I knew Truett, I offered to introduce them to each other. I hosted a dinner party for them at my house, and it was a great night.

Please don't get the impression that you need to know someone famous to help others in this area. Sometimes it's as simple as introducing one friend to another or one business associate to another. Just make connections. Be the bridge in people's relationships with others.

2. TAKE PEOPLE PLACES THEY CAN'T GO ON THEIR OWN

Early in our marriage, Margaret and I were dirt poor. Right out of college, I put in long hours for my career, and Margaret worked three jobs for us to make ends meet. We managed to get by, but there was no money left over for luxuries, such as vacations. Fortunately, I had an older brother who loved us and took care of us. The first five or six years of my professional life, any vacation we took was at the invitation of Larry and his wife Anita.

For the decade after that, our opportunities to go new places and have our horizons stretched were very limited. The only times I got to do something of value to me, it was because someone invited me. I could not have attended ball games, played golf courses, visited churches, attended conferences, and traveled to other countries without benefitting from the kindness of others. Later as Margaret and I enjoyed financial stability, it became our delight to take others places they would not have been able to go on their own.

You may have the power to give someone an experience that seems inaccessible to them. Start with your own family members. Take your children places they could not go on their own. There's no telling what kind of positive impact it will make. If you have the ability, expand the circle of people you help to friends, employees, and colleagues.

3. OFFER OPPORTUNITIES OTHERS CAN'T ATTAIN ON THEIR OWN

In the earlier part of my career when I possessed the desire to expand my speaking career, people helped me reach audiences I would never have had access to without their assistance. One of those people was Professor C. Peter Wagner of Fuller Seminary. Forty-five years ago, he invited me to speak to audiences of pastors around the country about leadership. He put me on a national stage for the first time and gave me credibility that I didn't possess on my own.

Few things are of greater value to a prepared person than an opportunity. Why? Because opportunities increase our potential. Demosthenes, the great orator of ancient Greece, said, "Small opportunities are often the beginning of great enterprises."[2] An opportunity seized is often the impetus for success. Help people win by giving them opportunities, and you will win with them.

4. SHARE IDEAS OTHERS WON'T DISCOVER ON THEIR OWN

What is an idea worth? Every product begins with an idea. Every service begins with an idea. Every business, every book, every new invention begins with an idea. Ideas are what make the world move forward. So when you give someone an idea, you give them a great gift. You may be helping them create a bridge to a better future.

> "Small opportunities are often the beginning of great enterprises."
>
> —DEMOSTHENES

One of the things I love about writing books is the process that it takes me through. It usually starts with a concept that I'm excited to teach. I get a few ideas down on paper, and then I call together a group of creative thinkers to help me test the concept, brainstorm ideas, and flesh out an outline. Every time we've done this, people have given me great ideas that I never would have come up with on my own. I have to say I'm very grateful.

One of the things I enjoy most about creative people is that they love ideas, and they always seem to have more coming. The more they give away, the more new ideas they seem to come up with. Creativity and generosity feed each other.

That's one of the reasons I'm never reluctant to share ideas with others. I'm convinced that I will run out of time long before I run out of ideas. It's better to give some away and contribute to another person's success than to have them lying dormant in me.

We live in a world where people would rather build walls than bridges. They would rather divide people than bring them together. When you become a bridge-building leader, you really stand out from the crowd because it shows you're more interested in helping others than helping yourself. What an attractive quality that is.

PART 3

BECOME INTERESTING
TO PEOPLE

DO EVERYTHING WITH EXCELLENCE

I do the very best I know how—the very best I can;
and I mean to keep on doing so until the end.

—ABRAHAM LINCOLN

For years I've been invited to be the keynote speaker for organizations at special events. It's something I really enjoy. Communicating to an audience energizes me. It would be easy for me to "wing it" or do a canned speech that I have done elsewhere before. But I don't do that because it would not serve them well. Instead, I spend time researching the company. I find out as much as I can about the particular event they've planned and what they desire to accomplish. Why do I go to such trouble when I wouldn't necessarily need to? I do it because I have a goal every time I speak. Not only do I want the audience to walk away after I'm done communicating feeling informed and inspired; I want the person who invited me to speak at the event to say, "You exceeded our expectations." I want to deliver for them, and then some.

I admire and am attracted to people who are excellent at what they do, aren't you? It doesn't matter whether the person is great at leadership, painting, cooking, sports, woodworking, sculpture, singing, or finance. A person who hones their talent to the absolute best of their ability and uses it to benefit others has charisma.

HOW TO GIVE YOUR BEST EVERY TIME

Perhaps you are someone who already possesses an offer-your-best mindset. You do everything that matters with excellence. If so, I commend you, and I want to encourage you to maintain that attitude. If not, I want to help you. Embrace these four truths to help you improve:

1. EVERY DAY DESERVES YOUR BEST

More than thirty years ago I memorized a quote that has shaped the way I live: "My potential is God's gift to me. What I do with my potential is my gift to Him." I believe I am accountable to God, others, and myself for every gift, talent, resource, and opportunity I have in life. If I give less than my best, then I am shirking my responsibility.

UCLA basketball coach John Wooden was famous for his dedication to personal growth and high standard of excellence in everything he did. He practiced it in his personal life, brought it into his coaching routine, and instilled it in his players. One of his favorite sayings was "Make every day your masterpiece."[1] That's a great goal for each of us. If we give our very best all the time, we can

> "My potential is God's gift to me. What I do with my potential is my gift to Him."

make our lives into something special. And that will overflow into the lives of others.

2. EVERYONE IS IMPORTANT ENOUGH TO BE GIVEN YOUR BEST

We are most likely to give our best to those we love and respect. I think back to my days in school, and I remember loving some teachers and having others who left me cold. I always did my best for the teachers I liked, and for the others I did only what was needed to get a grade. Later, I realized that my off-and-on efforts frequently hurt my relationships with others as well as my potential for success. But then I discovered the antidote: if I saw *everyone* as important—not just the people I liked the most—I would always offer my very best. That change in attitude prompted a change in my actions.

I've made this point before, but it bears repeating. Everyone has value and deserves to be valued. When we keep this in mind, we are more likely to treat them with the respect they deserve and give them our best.

3. ANYTHING ORDINARY CAN BE MADE EXTRAORDINARY WITH EXCELLENCE

Most moments in life become special only if we treat them that way. The average day is average only because we don't make it something more. The most excellent way to elevate an experience is to give it our best. That makes it special. An average conversation becomes something better when you listen with great interest. A common relationship transforms when you give it uncommon effort. An unremarkable event becomes something special when you spice it up with creativity. You can make anything more important by giving your best to it.

What ordinary tasks can you improve by doing them with excellence? Can you make the school run with your kids into something special for them? Can you turn a team meeting from a tedious necessity into an experience that adds value to attendees? Can you spend time preparing spectacular questions for your mentor so that the time you spend together becomes life-changing for both of you? If you put your creativity to work and make these things extraordinary, the people you impact will long remember it.

4. PERFORMING WITH EXCELLENCE MAKES YOU EXTRAORDINARY

As you go about your normal activities, how often do the people you interact with perform at their highest level. If you go out to eat at a restaurant, what percentage of the time is your server extraordinary? One in ten? One in twenty? How about the food? Let's face it, many people are satisfied with average. They give just enough to get by, and no more. However, when you encounter someone who does their work with excellence—whether they're working as a server, bank teller, carpenter, dry cleaner, or customer service representative—they really stand out as extraordinary. Keep yourself to that same high standard of excellence in what you do, especially in your leadership, and you will stand out too.

There's a story I love about President Dwight Eisenhower. He once told the National Press Club that he regretted not having a better political background so that he would be a better orator. He said his lack of skill in that area reminded him of his boyhood days in Kansas when an old farmer had a cow for sale. The buyer asked the farmer about the cow's pedigree, butterfat production, and monthly production of milk. The farmer said, "I don't know what a pedigree is, and I don't have an idea about butterfat production, but she's a good cow, and she'll give you all the milk she has." That's all any of us can do—give all that we have. That's always enough. And it's always attractive.

19

BE A GENEROUS PERSON

Life's most persistent and urgent question
is, What are you doing for others?

—MARTIN LUTHER KING JR.

One of the most appealing qualities a leader can have is generosity. When someone gives to others—with no strings attached—it really makes them feel special. Jesuit theologian Pierre Teilhard de Chardin said, "The most satisfying thing in life is to have been able to give a large part of one's self to others."

Anyone who has unselfishly helped another person knows this to be true. Yet not everyone is able to adopt an ongoing mindset of giving toward others. Why is that? First of all, I believe it has nothing to do with circumstances. I've met generous people with almost nothing who were willing to share what little they possessed. And I've met wealthy people who were stingy with their time, money, and talents. The issue is really attitude.

THE SECRET TO BEING GENEROUS

Because generosity is an attitude issue, and attitude is a choice, it means anyone can become generous if they have the desire.

You can become a generous leader, which will not only benefit all the people you lead, but it will also make you more appealing as a leader. Who isn't attracted to a genuinely generous person who gives with no strings attached?

I've found that generosity in people almost always boils down to three characteristics. I encourage you to embrace them.

1. ADOPT AN ABUNDANCE MENTALITY

If you've read Stephen Covey's book *The Seven Habits of Highly Effective People*, then you are familiar with the concepts related to scarcity and abundance mindsets. In a nutshell, people with a scarcity mindset believe that in life, there's only a limited supply of anything to go around, whether it's money, resources, opportunity, and so forth. They see the world as a pie with a limited number of slices. Once those slices are gone, they're gone. As a result, people with a scarcity mindset fight to get their piece, and once they have it, they protect it. If those scarcity-minded people are particularly greedy and powerful, they may try to get *all* the pieces.[1]

People possessing an abundance mindset think quite differently. They believe there is plenty of everything to go around. If life is a pie, and others are helping themselves to pieces, the solution of the person with the abundance mindset is to find or bake another pie. There are always additional ways to make money, more or different resources to be discovered and employed, additional opportunities to be pursued. An old solution isn't working anymore? Don't worry: someone will find a new one. A natural resource is running low? No problem: a creative person will think of a new way of doing things that doesn't require that resource at all. The inventors, entrepreneurs, and explorers of the world are continually creating new "pies" so that everyone can get a slice.

People who habitually give with no strings attached almost always have an abundance mentality. They are generous because they believe that if they give, they will not run out of resources. Pastor and former college professor Henri Nouwen stated, "When we refrain from giving, with a scarcity mentality, the little we have will become less. When we give generously, with an abundance mentality, what we give away will multiply."

> "When we refrain from giving, with a scarcity mentality, the little we have will become less. When we give generously, with an abundance mentality, what we give away will multiply."
>
> —HENRI NOUWEN

I have found this to be true. Someone once asked me why he should adopt an abundance mentality, and he was surprised by my answer. I told him that if you believe in abundance, that's what life gives you. If you believe in scarcity, then that's what you get. I don't know why that is, but after sixty years of paying attention to people's attitudes and watching how life unfolded for them, I know it to be true. So, if you desire to be more generous, change your thinking and your attitude when it comes to abundance. Not only will it allow you to be more generous, but also it will change your life.

2. BECOME A MAKER INSTEAD OF A TAKER

Where do you focus your attention? With what mindset do you approach every day? I've observed that people go out into the world each morning with one of two intentions: taking or making. There's a great difference between the two.

Takers are people who take, grab, and consume whatever they can to meet their own needs. They look for leverage over others. They beat up others to get the best deal. They take without any thought of giving back. The worst of takers cheat others or steal from them. They see life as a rat race. Of course, the main problem with that is that even if you win, you're still a rat.

Makers, on the other hand, are people who give, create, and make things happen. They are looking for ways to add value to others. They like a fair trade, but they want to give first. Their focus is on others and making sure *they* get a fair deal first. Their focus is on creating progress for their team, colleagues, and organization. They desire and foster success for others. They want to create more for everyone.

Which are you: a maker or taker? As you start your day, are you focused on the seeds you're sowing? Or do you care about only the harvest you're reaping? To be a generous person, focus on sowing and you will receive a harvest in time. And those you lead with will be glad to work with you.

3. SEE THE BIG PICTURE

People who give to others are usually aware of the help *they* have received along the way. They recognize that they are standing on the shoulders of previous generations. The progress they make is due, at least in part, to the work and sacrifice of those who have gone before them. Because of this, they are determined to do for the next generation what was done for them.

Many years ago I came across a poem by Will Allen Dromgoole called "The Bridge Builder." I've always loved it because it beautifully illustrates a leader's desire to be generous and make the world better for those who follow him:

> An old man going a lone highway,
> Came, at the evening cold and gray,
> To a chasm vast and deep and wide.
> Through which was flowing a sullen tide
> The old man crossed in the twilight dim,

The sullen stream had no fear for him;
But he turned when safe on the other side
And built a bridge to span the tide.

"Old man," said a fellow pilgrim near,
"You are wasting your strength with building here;
Your journey will end with the ending day,
You never again will pass this way;
You've crossed the chasm, deep and wide,
Why build this bridge at evening tide?"

The builder lifted his old gray head;
"Good friend, in the path I have come," he said,
"There followed after me to-day
A youth whose feet must pass this way.
This chasm that has been as naught to me
To that fair-haired youth may a pitfall be;
He, too, must cross in the twilight dim;
Good friend, I am building this bridge for him!"[2]

To become better givers, we need greater perspective. When we realize how much we have benefited from the kindness of others, it becomes much easier for us to be generous.

One of the best things about being a generous person

is that it's so rewarding. College president and educational reformer Horace Mann commented, "We must be purposely kind and generous or we miss the best part of existence. The heart that goes out of itself gets large and full of joy. This is the great secret of the inner life. We do ourselves the most good doing something for others."[3]

BECOME A GOOD STORYTELLER

The universe is made of stories, not of atoms.

—MURIEL RUKEYSER

I'm a great admirer of President Abraham Lincoln. What a great leader! I've read that the "elite" of his time often criticized him for telling too many stories. They considered him to be unsophisticated. But he didn't let their opinion stop him, because he knew what connected with people and moved them. Lincoln remarked, "They say I tell a great many stories; I reckon I do, but I have found in the course of a long experience that common people, take them as they run, are more easily informed through the medium of a broad illustration than in any other way, and as to what the hypercritical few may think, I don't care."[1]

Like most people, I have a great appreciation for good stories and good storytellers. I've studied them and learned as much as I can from them. In the fall of 1999, Margaret and I took some friends to the small town of Jonesborough, Tennessee, to attend the annual National Storytelling Festival. More than seven thousand people from all over the country, many at considerable expense, came there to sit for hours on end on blankets, on folding chairs, sometimes even in the rain, to hear some of the best storytellers in the nation.

For days we watched one storyteller after another captivate their audience. The stories were diverse—sad, happy, funny, sentimental, historical, fictitious, mythical. Some had a great message; others simply entertained. But all the stories and storytellers had one thing in common: they had the power to captivate their listeners.

At the end of the conference, my friends and I discussed why these storytellers were so effective. "What traits did they have that made them so successful?" we asked. Here's the list we came up with:

- **Enthusiasm**—They enjoyed what they were doing and expressed themselves with joy and vitality.
- **Animation**—The presentations were marked by lively movement, facial expressions, and gestures.
- **Audience participation**—Nearly every storyteller involved the audience in some way, asking listeners to sing, clap, repeat phrases, or do sign language.
- **Spontaneity**—The storytellers adapted their communication to their listeners.
- **Memorization**—They told their stories without notes, freeing them up to maintain eye contact.
- **Humor**—Nearly every storyteller interjected humor in both serious and sad stories.
- **Creativity**—They communicated classic themes, but they delivered them from a fresh perspective.

- **Personal**—Most storytellers used the first person to make their stories more immediate.
- **Heartwarming**—Their stories made people feel good just having heard them.

Storytelling is very effective one-on-one, in small group conversation, and in front of large audiences. Invariably, the person who tells the best stories becomes the one to whom others turn their attention. Good storytellers are charismatic. Great storytellers are magnetic.

HOW TO TELL A GOOD STORY

Storytelling is an important tool for leaders. It is a skill that comes with practice, and fortunately, anyone can learn to develop it. If you don't have much experience with it, or you would like to improve, then allow me to give you a few tips:

SHARE SOMETHING YOU'VE EXPERIENCED

The stories we tell the best are the ones we've lived. We care about them, we know the material, and we know how they have affected us. And because they are ours, we can shape and embellish them any way we want. Everybody has had experiences that others would be interested in.

Think about the times in your life when something dramatic, frightening, heart-warming, or funny happened to you. What was the suspenseful moment at the center of the story? What do you need to say to set it up? What is the punchline or payoff? You want the whole story to build to that. After you've thought these ideas through, start working out how to tell it. The best stories relay everything needed for the story with style and emotion while leaving out anything unnecessary.

> **The stories we tell the best are the ones we've lived.**

Once you believe you have an approach for telling the story, try it out on someone. Pay attention to how they react. When were they most engaged? If you started to lose their attention, where in the story did that happen? Did they respond to the punchline the way you hoped? Make adjustments to it and tell it again. Keep improving it and telling it to new people until you get the results you desire. The way to become a good storyteller is to start out as a bad one and keep working to improve.

TELL STORIES WITH THE GOAL OF CONNECTING

The people who have the toughest time telling stories are the ones who try to impress others with them. If that describes you, then change your goal. Impressing people is difficult. Instead, tell stories with the purpose of connecting with people. Put the focus on the listener, and your storytelling skills will improve overnight.

PUT YOUR HEART INTO IT

People love humor, but not everyone can tell a funny story. If you can, go with it. But never underestimate the power of a story from the heart. If you want evidence, look at the sales figures of the *Chicken Soup for the Soul* books! Almost anyone can share a story that connects emotionally. If you want to tell a connecting story, make it warm. Put your heart into it. And don't be afraid to show people that you care about what you're talking about.

ASSUME THAT OTHERS WANT TO HEAR IT

One of the biggest mistakes novice storytellers make is being tentative. Nothing makes a story go flat more quickly than a timid delivery. If you're going to tell a story, be bold. Be energetic. Be engaging. Go for it, or don't go at all.

Good stories can be long or short, true or fictional, personal or sweeping. I love telling brief stories that have one of the four *H*s: heart, hope, humor, or help. I also love telling elaborate tales of adventures I've been on, like when I talked myself and three family members onto the Old Course in Scotland without a scheduled tee time. Or the story of how

I encouraged my nephew Eric to score his first home run in Little League.

Painter Benjamin West used to tell a story about himself as a boy. He said when his mother left the house, he would get out the oils and try to paint. One day when he pulled out paints, brushes, paper, and other supplies, he made a terrible a mess. When he realized his mother would be home soon, he tried desperately to get everything cleaned up, but he didn't make it. When she walked into the room, he prepared for the worst.

But, West said, what his mom did next completely surprised him. She picked up his painting, looked at it, and said, "My, what a beautiful painting of your sister." She gave him a kiss on the cheek and walked away. With that kiss, West said, he became a painter.[2]

What stories can you tell to connect with people, help them, and inspire them? The better you become at telling stories, the more it will help you to communicate with others and lead them. Through stories you can cast vision, break tension, teach skills, rally people, and build organizations. Great storytellers are relatable, charming, and charismatic. Work to become one.

21

HELP PEOPLE WIN

The most important measure of how good a game I played
was how much better I'd made my teammates play.

—BILL RUSSELL, WINNER OF MORE NBA
CHAMPIONSHIPS THAN ANY OTHER PLAYER

What's the greatest way to connect with people, develop rapport with them, and make yourself likeable to them? Help them win! Everybody loves to win, and everybody appreciates people who help them do it.

In the previous chapter, I mentioned that I used to tell a story about helping my nephew Eric score his first home run in Little League. In conferences, I'd take a full ten minutes relating the story of how Eric was petrified facing Butch the pitcher and took three strikes on three pitches without even swinging the bat. He walked away dejected. I went over and encouraged Eric, and I explained that his only job was to swing the bat. On his third at-bat, Eric swung the bat and accidentally got a hit. I of course coached him all the way around the bases and slid into home plate with him.

OK, so maybe I embellished the story a bit when I told it. But here's what's true. He really did get a hit, I really did tell him to keep running, and he did score. And what's more, he fell in love with baseball and played it the whole time when he was growing up. And when he finished high school, he made it a point to come visit me, reminisce about that first game, and give me the news he would be going to college on a baseball scholarship. And he gave me credit for being a small part of that. That really touched my heart.

WHAT IT TAKES TO HELP OTHERS WIN

Helping another person to win is one of the greatest feelings in the world. I haven't met a person yet who doesn't like to win. And everyone I know who's made the effort to help others has said that it is the most rewarding part of life. As poet Ralph Waldo Emerson said, "It is one of the most beautiful compensations of life that no man can sincerely try to help another without helping himself."[1]

> "It is one of the most beautiful compensations of life that no man can sincerely try to help another without helping himself."
>
> —RALPH WALDO EMERSON

If you want to help people win, you can do so by taking the following steps:

BELIEVE IN PEOPLE

If you want to help people win, you have to believe in them, and you have to believe they can. One time after a leadership conference, a man came up to me and asked a pointed question: "How do I get unbelievable results from a person?" My answer: "Have unbelievable expectations about that person."

If you don't believe in people, then you are unlikely to do everything you can to help them win. People know when someone doesn't believe in them. They see right through pretense and insincere backslapping. But when they know you genuinely believe in them, magic begins to happen. What writer John Spalding said is true: "Those who believe in our ability do more than stimulate us. They create for us an atmosphere in which it becomes easier to succeed."

GIVE PEOPLE HOPE

A reporter asked Prime Minister Winston Churchill, who led Britain during the Second World War, what was the greatest weapon his country possessed against the Nazi regime of Hitler. Without pausing for even a moment, Churchill said, "It is what England's greatest weapon has always been—hope."

Hope is one of the most powerful and energizing words in the English language. It is something that gives us power to keep going in the toughest of times. And that power energizes us with excitement and anticipation as we look toward the future.

It's been said that a person can live forty days without food, four days without water, four minutes without air, but only four seconds without hope. If you want to help people win, then become a purveyor of hope.

FOCUS ON THE PROCESS, NOT JUST THE WIN

Many of us desire the win so much that we forget what it takes to get there. We're like the kid who plays chess with his grandfather. When he loses, he says, "Oh no! Not again! Grampa, you always win!"

"What do you want me to do, lose on purpose?" the old man replies. "You won't learn anything if I do that!"

"I don't wanna learn anything," the boy says. "I just wanna win!"

That's the way we often feel, but let's be honest. We know most big successes are difficult and must be hard won. For that reason, we need to be willing to hang in there with others and help them until they achieve the win. By doing that, you're not only helping them attain the win; you're also teaching them and giving them the means for additional future victories. It's like the old adage: to feed someone for a day, give them a fish. To feed them for a lifetime, teach them to fish. And the only thing sweeter than a win is the ability to achieve a whole bunch of wins.

UNDERSTAND THAT WHEN YOU HELP OTHERS WIN, YOU ALSO WIN

In 1984, Lou Whittaker led the first all-American team to the summit of Mt. Everest. After months of grueling effort, five members of the team reached the final campsite at twenty-seven thousand feet. With two thousand feet to go, they met in a crowded tent. Whittaker had a tough decision to make: he knew how highly motivated all five climbers were to climb to the highest point on earth. But two would have to go back to the previous camp, load up food, water, and oxygen, then return to the camp where they now met. After completing this support assignment, these two climbers would be in no condition to make a try for the summit. The others would stay in the tent that day to drink water, breathe oxygen, and rest, preparing them for the summit attempt the next day.

The first decision Whittaker made was to stay at the twenty-seven-thousand-foot camp to coordinate the team's activities. The next was to send the two strongest climbers down the mountain to get the supplies; it was the tougher job. The two weaker climbers would rest, renew their strength, and receive the glory of the summit.

When asked why he didn't assign himself the summit run, his answer showed his understanding of people and the strength of his leadership. He said, "My job was to put other people on top."

Whittaker understood that when people make the right decisions, choosing to help the entire team to achieve its goal, everybody wins. You can't help winning when you help others win.

CONCLUSION

Connect with Charisma

There you have them: 21 skills you can use for connecting with people. Learn them, practice them, and enjoy their benefits. When you become interested in people, invested in people, and interesting to people, you will increase your influence, effectiveness, and impact as a leader.

I want to remind you to use these skills with the right motives. Never use them to manipulate people or get your way. If your goal is to look better than you really are or to climb the ladder, you've missed the point. Use these skills only to motivate others for their benefit and mutual advantage. If your goal is always to help people and lead them better, charisma will be the natural byproduct.

NOTES

INTRODUCTION

1. Mrs. C. B. Klein, "Entrance Exam," *The Reader's Digest*, Volume 74 (1959), 54, https://archive.org/details/dli.bengal.10689.12240/page/n517/mode/2up?q=entrance.

CHAPTER 1: PUT YOUR FOCUS ON OTHERS

1. John C. Maxwell, *Winning with People* (Nashville: Thomas Nelson, 2004), 59.

2. Zig Zigler, "Everyone's Definition of Success," Creators Syndicate, June 15, 2022, https://www.creators.com/read/classic-zig-ziglar/06/22/everyones-definition-of-success-b0a94.

CHAPTER 2: BELIEVE THE BEST OF OTHERS

1. Sal Marino, "Teams Are the Best Way to Highlight Stars," IndustryWeek Straight Talk, December 21, 2004, https://www.industryweek.com/talent/article/21946936/straight-talk.

2. John 8:9.

3. John G. Bennett, *The Crisis of Human Affairs* (London: Hodder and Stoughton, 1948).

4. David Augsburger, *Caring Enough to Forgive* (Raleigh, NC: Regal Books, 1981), 98.

5. Martin Luther King Jr., *Strength to Love* (Boston: Beacon Press, 1981), 33.

CHAPTER 3: ADD VALUE TO PEOPLE

1. Leslie T. Giblin, *How to Have Confidence and Power in Dealing with People* (Hoboken, NJ: Penguin, 1985), 32.

2. Sydney J. Harris, *Strictly Personal* (Washington, DC: Regnery Publishing, 1953), 30.

CHAPTER 4: ENCOURAGE OTHERS EVERY TIME YOU MEET

1. Leila Zenderland, *Measuring Minds: Henry Herbert Goddard and the Origins of American Intelligence Testing* (Cambridge: Cambridge University Press, 1998).

2. Jerry Kramer, ed., *Lombardi: Winning Is the Only Thing* (New York: World Publishing Company, 1976).

3. Jerry Kramer, ed., *Lombardi: Winning Is the Only Thing* (New York: World Publishing Company, 1976).

4. National Archives, "From Benjamin Franklin to John Paul Jones, 5 July 1780," accessed October 8, 2024, https://founders.archives.gov/documents/Franklin/01-33-02-0018.

CHAPTER 5: REMEMBER PEOPLE'S NAMES

1. Dwight Garner, "Classic Advice: Please, Leave Well Enough Alone," *New York Times*, October 5, 2011, https://www.nytimes.com/2011/10/05/books/books-of-the-times-classic-advice-please-leave-well-enough-alone.html.

2. Dale Carnegie, *How to Win Friends and Influence People: Updated for the Next Generation of Leaders* (New York: Simon and Schuster, 2022), 84 of 288, Kindle.

3. William Shakespeare, *Othello* (New York: Washington Square Press, 2004), act 3, sc. 3, p. 129.

4. Harry Lorayne and Jerry Lucas, *The Memory Book: The Classic Guide to Improving Your Memory at Work, School, and at Play* (New York: Ballantine Books, 2012).

CHAPTER 6: LEARN WHAT MATTERS TO PEOPLE

1. Florence Littauer, *Personality Plus* (Grand Rapids, MI: Fleming H. Revell, 1992).

2. J. Fred Bucy, *Dodging Elephants: The Autobiography of J. Fred Bucy*, ed. Kenneth R. Martin (Indianapolis, IN: Dog Ear Publishing, 2014).

CHAPTER 7: LISTEN WITH AN OPEN HEART

1. Woodrow Wilson, "Leaders of Men," in *Woodrow Wilson: The Essential Political Writings*, ed. Ronald J. Pestritto (Lanham, MD: Lexington Books, 2005), 211–230.

2. Herb Cohen, *You Can Negotiate Anything* (New York: Citadel Press, 1994), 217.

3. Michael Abrashoff, *It's Your Ship: Management Techniques from the Best Damn Ship in the Navy* (New York: Grand Central, 2012), 43 of 213, Kindle.

4. David D. Burns. AZQuotes.com, Wind and Fly LTD, 2024. https://www.azquotes.com/author/38006-David _D_Burns, accessed November 04, 2024.

5. David D. Burns. AZQuotes.com, Wind and Fly LTD, 2024. https://www.azquotes.com/quote/1403625, accessed November 04, 2024.

CHAPTER 9: EXPRESS HOW MUCH YOU VALUE SOMEONE

1. "Mary Kay Global," MaryKay.com, accessed June 14, 2024, https://www.marykay.com/en-us/about-mary-kay/mary-kay-around-the-world.

2. Willard Scott, *Willard Scott's Down Home Stories* (New York: Bobbs-Merrill, 1984), 96.

3. Captain D. Michael Abrashoff, *It's Your Ship* (New York: Warner Books, 2002), 146.

4. Charlie Wetzel, conversation with the author.

CHAPTER 10: BE QUICK TO HELP OTHERS

1. Zig Ziglar, *Zig Ziglar's Secrets of Closing the Sale* (Old Tappan, NJ: Fleming H. Revell, 1984), 22.

2. Frank Darabont, *Walking the Mile: A Behind-the-Scenes Documentary*, directed by Constantine Nasr (Burbank, CA: Warner Home Video, 2000).

3. Belden Lane, "Rabbinical Stories," *Christian Century*, 98, no. 41 (December 16, 1981).

4. Ken Sutterfield, *The Power of an Encouraging Word* (Green Forest, AR: New Leaf, 1997), 106.

CHAPTER 11: INVITE PEOPLE TO JOIN YOUR TEAM

1. Woodrow Wilson, "How It Feels to Be President,"

speech to the National Press Club at Washington, *The Independent* 77, March 20, 1914.

2. Lyndon B. Johnson, "About," LBJ Foundation, accessed October 9, 2024, https://www.lbjaward.org/about.html.

3. Charles Schulz, *Peanuts*, February 1, 1987, https://peanuts.fandom.com/wiki/February_1987_comic_strips.

4. Warren Bennis, *Managing People Is Like Herding Cats* (Provo, UT: Executive Excellence Publishing, 1997), 98.

5. Thomas J. Neff and James A. Citrin, *Lessons from the Top* (New York: Currency/Doubleday, 2001), 273.

CHAPTER 12: ENCOURAGE THE DREAMS OF OTHERS

1. Candice Bergen, *Knock Wood* (New York: Simon and Schuster, 2014), 155.

2. Benjamin Franklin, *Legendary Quotes of Benjamin Franklin*, edited by Screechinth C (Roosevelt, UT: UB Tech, 2016), 158.

3. Scott Adams, "My Greatest Lesson," *Fast Company*, June–July 1998, 83.

CHAPTER 13: SHARE THE CREDIT WITH OTHERS

1. R. Edward Turner, ed., *The Quotable Perot* (San Francisco: 24 Hour Books, 1992), 26.

2. Michael Benson, ed., *Winning Words: Classic Quotes from the World of Sports* (Lanham, MD: Taylor Trade Publishing, 2008), 205.

CHAPTER 14: CREATE SPECIAL MOMENTS FOR OTHERS

1. Lewis Carroll, *Through the Looking Glass* (Mineola: Dover Publications, 1999), 45.

2. John McCrone, "Don't Forget Your Memory Aide: Only 30 and Already You Can't Remember What Was Discussed at Last Week's Meeting? By the Time You Get Really Old and Forgetful, a Memory Prosthesis Could Be the Answer," *New Scientist*, February 5, 1994, https://institutions.newscientist.com/article/mg1411 9114-200/.

CHAPTER 15: SHARE INFORMATION WITH OTHERS

1. Charlie Wetzel, conversation with the author.

CHAPTER 16: SPEAK INTO PEOPLE'S LIVES

1. J. Sterling Livingston, *Pygmalion in Management* (Boston: Harvard Business School Publishing, 2009).

2. David Jeremiah, *The Power of Encouragement* (Sisters, OR: Multnomah Books, 1997).

3. Helen Mrosla, "All Good Things," in *Chicken Soup for the Soul: 101 Stories to Open the Heart and Rekindle the Spirit*, ed. Jack Canfield and Mark Victor Hansen (Deerfield Beach, FL: Health Communications, 1993), 125–128.

4. James C. Humes, *The Wit and Wisdom of Winston Churchill* (New York: Harper Perennial, 1994), 119–20.

CHAPTER 17: BUILD BRIDGES FOR OTHERS

1. Henry Van Dyke, *The Works of Henry Van Dyke: Counsels by the Way* (New York: Scribner and Sons, 1921), 129.

2. Susan Ratcliffe, ed., *Oxford Essential Quotations* (online: Oxford University Press, 2017), 162.

CHAPTER 18: DO EVERYTHING WITH EXCELLENCE

1. Craig Impelman, "John Wooden's 7-Point Creed: 'Be True to Yourself,'" Success, The Wooden Effect, December 13, 2016, https://www.thewoodeneffect.com /john-woodens-7-point-creed-true/?__hstc=71610892 .561dc547e81bf7445a791b80837a5003.1728585327116 .1728585327116.1728585327116.1&__hssc=71610892 .1.1728585327116&__hsfp=2091169197.

CHAPTER 19: BE A GENEROUS PERSON

1. Stephen Covey, *The Seven Habits of Highly Effective People* (New York: Free Press, 1989).

2. Will Allen Dromgoole, "The Bridge Builder," *Father: An Anthology of Verse* (New York: E.P. Dutton and Company, 1931), on Poetry Foundation website, accessed June 19, 2024, https://www.poetryfoundation.org/poems/52702/the-bridge-builder.

3. Carroll Simcox, ed., *3000 Quotations on Christian Themes* (Grand Rapids, MI: Baker Book House, 1989).

CHAPTER 20: BECOME A GOOD STORYTELLER

1. Alexander Thorndike Rice, ed., *Reminiscences of Abraham Lincoln by Distinguished Men of His Time* (New York: North American Publishing Company, 1886), 427–28.

2. John Galt, *The Life and Studies of Benjamin West, Esq.* (London: Royal Academy of London, 1817), 10–11; Richard W. Leeman, ed., *African-American Orators: A Bio-Critical Sourcebook* (Westport: Greenwood Publishing Group, 1996), 176.

CHAPTER 21: HELP PEOPLE WIN

1. Zig Ziglar, *The One Year Daily Insights with Zig Ziglar* (Carol Stream, IL: Tyndale Momentum, 2009), May 15 entry.

ABOUT THE AUTHOR

John C. Maxwell is a #1 *New York Times* bestselling author, speaker, coach, and leader who has sold more than 36 million books in fifty languages. He is the founder of Maxwell Leadership®—the leadership development organization created to expand the reach of his principles of helping people lead powerful, positive change. Maxwell's books and programs have been translated into 70 languages and have been used to train tens of millions of leaders in every nation. His work also includes that of the Maxwell Leadership Foundation and EQUIP, nonprofit organizations that have impacted millions of adults and youth across the globe through values-based, people-centric leadership training.

John has been recognized as the #1 leader in business by the American Management Association and as the world's most influential leadership expert by both *Business Insider* and *Inc.* magazine. He is a recipient of the Horatio Alger Award and the Mother Teresa Prize for Global Peace and Leadership from the Luminary Leadership Network.

Maxwell and the work of Maxwell Leadership continue to influence individuals and organizations worldwide—from *Fortune* 500 CEOs and national leaders to entrepreneurs and the leaders of tomorrow. For more information about him and Maxwell Leadership, visit MaxwellLeadership.com.

THE SELF-AWARE LEADER

THE SELF-AWARE LEADER

JOHN C. MAXWELL

Play to Your Strengths
and Unleash Your Team

Unlock your leadership potential with insights from *The Self-Aware Leader*. John Maxwell guides you to:

- Make impactful decisions.
- Correct your missteps.
- Elevate team dynamics.

Self-awareness is crucial for leaders to avoid micromanagement, gracefully handle criticism, and acknowledge team contributions. This book is your key to identifying strengths, honing learning skills, and becoming a more effective listener.

Read *The Self-Aware Leader* today and transform your approach to leadership through spiritual insights and empowerment.

LEADERSHIFT

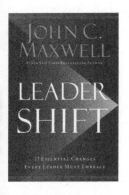

In *Leadershift: The 11 Essential Changes Every Leader Must Embrace*, leadership expert and bestselling author John C. Maxwell teaches how to accelerate your career by putting your leadership into high gear. Providing a blueprint for change, he shares the shifts he made during his long and successful career. Among those leadershifts are

- The Improvement Shift—from Team Uniformity to Team Diversity
- The Abundance Shift—from Maintaining to Creating
- The Reproduction Shift—from Ladder Climbing to Ladder Building
- The Impact Shift—from Trained Leaders to Transformational Leaders

Gain insight and guidance so that you can embrace these shifts and put them into action. Then stay ahead of the curve by not only relying on speed but thriving on timing, innovating, and making changes before they are necessary.

Instead of staying the course, you can change your trajectory and position yourself for new and exciting achievements.